Books by Andrew M. Greeley

THE FRIENDSHIP GAME

THE
FRIENDSHIP
GAME

ANDREW M. GREELEY

DOUBLEDAY & COMPANY, INC.

GARDEN CITY, NEW YORK

1970

For My Friend Eugene Kennedy

CONTENTS

"Trust ihvryone, Hinnissey,
but make sure the cards are cut."

WORDS OF MR. DOOLEY
(SEEN ON A PHOTOGRAPH IN THE OFFICE OF DANIEL PATRICK MOYNIHAN).

INTRODUCTION

This book is a series of reflective essays about the most pleasurable and most difficult of specifically human aitivities —friendship. That it is the most pleasurable, I think hardly needs to be documented. Philosophers, poets, and mystics down through the ages have extolled the merits of friendship. That it is the most difficult of the specifically human activities is a point to which the philosopher, poets, and mystics may allude to only in passing but, surely, it is obvious enough to anyone who has been involved in friendship. One is forced to conclude that successful friendship has been a relatively rare phenomenon in human history. Perhaps the ecstasy of the poets, the philosophers, and the mystics over friendship is in part rooted in their awareness of how rare it is.

Some recent social philosophers, particularly under the influence of the French thinker, Levi-Straus, have suggested that patterned human relationships come into being from their economic and structural utility and that interpersonal warmth and affection are a secondary result. The family came into being because it was useful for organizing work and for the effective rearing of children. Love between husband and wife was an almost accidental and unintended result. In other words, man stumbled into married friendship—and all other friendships—almost by chance. It was in very recent times that affection between husband and wife was considered to be important *before* marriage and indeed the only justification for beginning a marriage. Friendship as the binding power that will hold a man and woman together is a new discovery and one whose success is not yet validated. If it is not yet clear that friendship alone can keep a man and woman together, it is even less clear that friendship can exist in other human structures save as a very rare exception. But one of the major cultural events of our era is the determination of many men and women to build a new world in which friendship replaces fear and force as the fabric of human society.

It is a truism that man is a complex, not to say convoluted creature, but one realizes how intricate are the complexities and how twisted the convolutions when one begins to analyze that human relationship we call friendship. The urge to be oneself for the other is an overwhelmingly powerful human urge, and yet, the resistance built into the personality against the urge is equally powerful. Man is driven toward friendship and repelled from it by the primordial forces of his personality. Any creature who manages to get himself caught in such a trap has to be complex and convoluted.

There is, therefore, in this book a good deal about the difficulties of friendship. The writer is neither a poet nor a philosopher nor a mystic but, alas for him, a social scientist; it is the nature of the profession that the social scientist goes around looking for difficulties. However, one advantage of having him comment on friendship is that he has some tools that may help the rest of us think a little more clearly about the problems and the challenges of friendship.

Although friendship is a painful task, it is a mistake, I think, to overemphasize the pain and to forge that the payoff is greater than the pain. To be a professional football quarterback is not exactly easy, and yet there are tens of thousands, and perhaps hundreds of thousands, of males in our republic who on Sunday afternoon during the autumn would give anything if they could be one; most of the great quarterbacks are singularly reluctant to retire from the game no matter how fierce the pounding they receive from gentlemen like Merlin Olsen or Roger Brown. Similarly, climbing mountains is, I am told, a difficult, demanding, painful, and exhausting enterprise. Yet those who engage in such behavior reportedly enjoy it immensely. Man is a playful animal, and he chooses for his games those forms of play that provide the greatest challenge. Part of the payoff of friendship is that it is such a challenging and demanding game.

The most depressing part of the friendship game is that one can lose. Friendships can come to an end, at least up to a certain point in their development. The attempts that we and the other make to be ourselves for one another can be frustrated, perhaps by my weakness, perhaps by his, or perhaps by an inevitable and immutable mismatch of our personality characteristics. A relationship that seemed so promising, that had so much warmth and so much joy, is aborted before it comes to fulfillment. We have taken risks and have lost. We have offered ourselves and been rejected, or have offered ourselves and then found it was necessary to withdraw the offer. It doesn't take many such experiences to persuade us that friendship is risky and perhaps too risky.

On the other hand, if we are not willing to run risks we are certainly never going to have friendships; friendships can only occur, as we shall suggest in the chapters of this book, when we offer ourself to the other, and to offer ourself to someone else is the most risky of all human endeavors.

The second great agony of the friendship quest is the necessity of maintaining a profound respect for our own integrity and value in the friendship relationship. If friendship is not possible unless we offer ourself, neither is it possible unless we respect that self that we offer. To have such respect flies in the face of all the fears, anxieties, and low self-esteem that beset us. We become strong through friendship and yet, paradoxically, we cannot even attempt friendship unless we are strong. He who leads in the friendship game out of weakness is depending on his partner to be holding strong cards, and anyone who has played bridge knows what that kind of a lead will do to a relationship. Friendship demands self-surrender, but it does not mean the surrender of our integrity or our dignity. Quite the contrary, if we lose ourself in the relationship there is no self to surrender.

The paradox of friendship, then, of risk-taking rooted in self-respect and strength, of giving and surrendering ourself while never losing our dignity and integrity, is the principal theme upon which we will meditate in the essays in this book. My reflections are based in part on traditional wisdom (of the Catholic Christian variety), in part on the insights of social science, and in part—as is necessary in any book on the subject—on my own experience.

It is, I suppose, inevitable that a good deal of my personality will be revealed, perhaps more than I would want. Although I don't propose to talk about myself much in this volume (that sort of thing can be saved for eventual memoirs), it should be noted that there are both advantages and disadvantages for a Catholic priest in writing a book about friendship, advantages and disadvantages that have precious little to do with the celibate state. Having been trained to believe that friendship was something that he was not to be permitted, and then making the discovery in middle years, after the Vatican Council, that friendship was at the very core of the Christian message ("by this all men shall know that you are my disciples, that you have love for one another"), the priest can at least view the friendship process from a somewhat different perspective from other observers.

He may also be more inclined to see friendship from a religious perspective than would other observers. Even though the present volume is not explicitly religious and does not presume that the reader shares the writer's Catholic Christian commitments, there is no escaping the fact that it is necessarily a religious work, for friendship is religious behavior in the primordial sense of that word. In the friendship relation we give of *ourselves,* and such an offering of the totality of our being is so primordial and intimate that it touches the very roots of our existence and forces us necessarily to face questions of the ultimate. That most intimate of friendships—the marriage union—has always been shrouded in religious ceremonial not so much because religion had wanted to dominate marriage as because the marriage exchange of gifts cannot help but be religious.

However, friendship need not be explicitly religious, and this book will assume, for the sake of discussion, that questions of formalized and explicit religious commitment are left aside. Nevertheless, I will fall back on words like faith and hope, whose religious overtones are impossible to exclude.

Finally, it is expected of an author to acknowledge the gratitude he owes to those who have helped him write a book. What little I know about friendship I have learned both painfully and joyously with the help of others. To the men and women, therefore, who have been my friends, in good times and in bad times, in hope and in fear, in faith and in anxiety, in expectation and in discouragement, in separation and in love, I hereby express my thanks.

A faithful friend is a sure shelter,
    whoever finds one has found a rare treasure.
A faithful friend is something beyond price,
    there is no measuring his worth.
A faithful friend is the elixir of life,
    and those who fear the Lord will find one.
Whoever fears the Lord makes true friends,
    for as a man is, so is his friend.

—ECCLESIASTICUS 6:14–17

THE FRIENDSHIP GAME

1

FRIENDSHIP AS INVITATION, GIFT, AND PROMISE

Man is essentially a lonely creature. He is one of the few animals who would like to leave his pack if he could; but he also has powerful urges and instincts toward unity with his fellows. Perhaps it is his gift of reflection, his consciousness about himself, his realization of his own finite destiny, his awareness that he must someday die. But man is ill at ease with his fellows. He is the only animal who is capable of wondering what others think about him, or caring whether others like him. He is also the only animal who wants others to think well of him and wants others to like him and, thus, inevitably and necessarily, the only one who can be afraid that others do not think well of him and do not like him.

If he could, man would like to be free of the others, able to exist without them, able, like the late Alan Ladd in the by now legendary movie, *Shane,* to ride off toward the mountains leaving human intimacy behind. There is something so admirably cool and antiseptic about Shane, particularly since the little boy dashes after him pathetically screaming his name. Shane leaves not because he is rejected by others and, indeed, despite their affection for him. He leaves rather because he is strong enough to be sufficient unto himself; but, while we admire Shane riding off toward the mountains, we still feel sorry for him because we know that it is his destiny to be alone. On occasion, we would like that to be our own destiny, but it's much better to enjoy it vicariously. We would like to be alone, but we really don't want to be alone.

Jean-Paul Sartre has suggested that hell is other people. It is, but so too is heaven.

Friendship is a breakthrough in the walls that men build up to separate them from others. It is a yielding to man's instincts toward unity with his fellows and a conquering of those instincts that incline him to turn away from his fellows. Friendship is Shane reversing his horse and riding back to the ranch. Friendship is our successful conquest of fear of the other.

It is fear, therefore, that is the principal barrier to friendship and fear ultimately for our life. The others, whoever they may be, may destroy us, mutilate us, cut us off, drop us. The primary human fear is the fear of falling, the only fear that the infant has, and fear to which all other fears are assimilated as we learn them. The fear of falling is neurological, but with the passage of time it is overlaid with psychological fears. Man does not want to trust himself to his fellow men because he is afraid if he leaves himself open to others, the others will kill him—either physically or emotionally.

The philosopher Hobbes raised the question of how human society is possible, and concluded rather pessimistically that it is not. Most philosophers since then really haven't been able to respond adequately to the Hobbesian question. Human society isn't possible, but it somehow or the other exists, though at times, just barely. The laws, the conventions, the mores that hold us together in human community are nothing more than a thin red line we use to hold terror at bay. Fear, suspicion, distrust, anger well up within the personality of each one of us, and we frequently feel that we must either kill or be killed. The violence, the crime, the warfare that have been part of the human condition since the beginning manifest what a primordially antisocial being man is and how deep is his fear and suspicion of others. It took a long time for us to develop complex societies and, as Hobbes quite correctly pointed out, most such societies were held together by force and power. More recently, the human race has attempted democratic societies in which men join together with their fellows on the basis of free consensus, more or less. The present stresses and strains in the society of the American republic as conflicting voices threaten to tear apart the fabric of society are conclusive evidence of how difficult a consensual community really is. We are, it would seem, but one step away from terror—just barely out of the jungle. Man has indeed come down from the trees and perhaps ventured even to the edge of the plain, but he still has in his arms a large stack of bananas with which he is ready to pelt passers-by.

Friendship, then, is man's attempt to transcend the boundaries of terror.

It is first of all an *invitation*. Friendship says to the other, "Come with me. There's nothing to be afraid of. Let us put aside our foolish fears and terrors. Let us tear down the barrier between us. Let us pledge ourselves not to destroy or mutilate one another but rather to comfort, challenge, and support. Let us speak honestly and openly with one another. Let us trust. Let us set up bonds that will hold us together. Let us make a commitment to one another. Let us establish very clearly the conditions that we both will honor in our friendship."

Essential to this invitation is assuring the other that he need not be afraid of us, that, whatever other terrors may assail him, in his relationship with us he need have no terror. It is a difficult message to convey. Most of us are shocked to learn that we terrify others even though we are all too painfully aware that others terrify us. We think that terror is our monopoly and that others do not share it. We do not see terror in the eyes of others partly because they are so quick to cover it up—frequently with hatred—but also because we are afraid to admit to ourselves that we see it. Nevertheless, there are occasional instances when we can see terror in someone else's eyes, and this is a profoundly disturbing experience. Frequently, the terror flashes through the eyes of someone whom we would have thought immune from fear, and surely from fear of us. Why should a successful professor be afraid of his students? Why should a perfectly secure superior be frightened by a subordinate? Why should a strong, vigorous, successful male be afraid of a frail, apparently defenseless woman? Why should a powerful master be afraid of a weak servant? And yet, on occasion, the slave realizes that he is the master; the student, that he is the teacher; the subordinate, that he is the superior; and the woman understands that with a slight change of facial expression she could destroy the seemingly powerful male whom she actually holds in the palm of her hand.

But why should the other be afraid of us? He is the one that has the strength and we are the ones who are weak. His defenses are superb and ours are pitiful. He could easily overwhelm us and he is frightened of us. Good Lord, he is as frightened of us as we are of him!

We want to tell the other that as far as we are concerned, his terror is foolish. There is no one in the world less likely to want to hurt him and no one in the world more likely to want to make him happy. We want to tell him that we are as afraid of him as he is of us. We want to be able to laugh together with him at our silly, foolish, mutual fears. We want to protest the utter absurdity of the thought that we would hurt him. We want to pledge ourselves to him, to protect him from others who might injure him. We want to assure him that our momentary glimpse of his vulnerability makes him even more pleasurable to us.

But we generally do not do any of these things. We are embarrassed to discover our power over him and afraid to embarrass him by indicating that we are aware of our power. Terror establishes a bond between us and him, a bond that may make demands on both of us. We would rather paper over terror with a cliché that will enable us both to escape from the raw and primordial passion that suddenly sprang up between us in that fleeting instant when we saw in his eyes the look of the haunted animal awaiting death.

Friendship, then, is an invitation to put aside terror. It involves, however implicitly, an acknowledgment that we and the other are afraid of each other but are willing, temporarily and provisionally, to act as though we were not afraid, and perhaps even to acknowledge to one another the fears when they are especially powerful. The invitation to friendship says to the other, "I will actually let you see me be afraid of you if you will let me see you being afraid of me."

Friendship is also a *gift*. Indeed, it is essentially and primarily a gift.

In order that we might persuade the other to accept our invitation, we offer him an inducement, that is to say, we offer him ourself. We say to the other, "I will give you me, I will not hold back, I will not hide, I will put myself at your service, will be willing to listen and to support, to run the risk of being hurt. I am yours to do with as you want, but my faith in you is so great that I know I have nothing to fear from you."

Such a gift does not, initially at least, eliminate terror, and it probably never completely eliminates it no matter how powerful the friendship grows. On the contrary, it frankly acknowledges the terror but dismisses it as irrelevant. It says in effect, "I want you so badly that I am prepared to ignore my terror and offer myself to you. I am even willing to be confident enough of my own attractiveness as a gift to believe—despite all the overwhelming evidence I have to the contrary—that you will find me irresistible and even put aside your terror—which is obviously completely unfounded —and give yourself to me in return. You are so irresistible to me that I am willing to risk my irresistibility by giving myself to you."

There is nothing more difficult for man to do than to make such a gift. If only he could give it once and not have to do it again. But friendship is not a single gift; it is rather a constant renewal. That is why it becomes easier through practice. The giving of one's self to the other, no matter how much love exists, is always a challenging, risky affair because it is always a leap in the face of terror.

The gift is not a disinterested one. The ancient argument among philosophers and theologians about "pure" love, that is to say, a love in which the lover sought nothing for himself, was a foolish one. George Berrnannos' heroes who, in line with Archbishop Fenolon's teaching, were willing even to rejoice in their own damnation, if it were God's will, turned out to be very disturbed human beings. The gift of one's self to another is unselfish in the sense that we are willing to entrust ourself to another without consciously holding back any part of ourself. But it is not, and cannot be, unselfish in the sense that we want nothing in return.

Martin D'Arcy, in his brilliant *Mind and Heart of Love,* resolves the philosophical debate about "pure love" by saying that, in the final analysis, the desire of the lover is not to possess the beloved but to be possessed by the beloved. But we realize that when we are possessed by our beloved, in that very same act we also possess. Friendship, then, is, quite finally, an exchange relation. We give ourselves because we want the other.

Similarly, the Scholastic argument about the love of benevolence and the love of concupiscence is, from the point of view of the psychodynamics of human relationships, a merely verbal argument. Of course we want our friend to be happy because he is good and wonderful and deserves happiness. Indeed, we are willing to give ourself to him to enhance his happiness, but we want him to give himself to us in return to enhance our happiness. In effect, we dismiss any statement of the issue that opposes our happiness to the beloved's happiness. Friendship assumes rather that the two of us will be happier together than we will be separately. Our selfishness is necessarily selfless and our unselfishness is necessarily self-seeking. We are unselfish to make the other happy, and we are selfish because we know his happiness will make us happier.

But however enlightened the selfishness of our gift-giving may be, however wise an exchange decision it is, however shrewd an investment in the marketplace of happiness it may turn out to be, it is not our money or our talent or our ambitions or our hopes that we are investing, it is ourself, our masculinity or femininity, our basic humanity. The ultimate human paradox is that we cannot be human unless we are willing to risk our humanity.

Finally, friendship is a *promise.* It is a promise to ecstasy, a dream of pleasure and joy, a utopian vision. It is a promise of a wonderland in which we shall forever play together. When I offer myself in friendship to you I promise that the best in me will become better and better and that I will demand of you that the best in you become better and better. As the fear and the anxiety, the suspicion and distrust in the two of us melt away, the world in which we live will grow more splendid, and together we shall frolic in that world. It is not merely myself that I promise to you without condition and without limit but it is a whole environment in which the two of us will become happier and happier that I offer to you, and of course you make the same promise back to me.

Friendship is a combination of conquest and surrender. We win the other by surrendering ourself to him. We get the other by giving ourself to him and he, in his turn, conquers us by surrendering to us. Surrender, as we have said before, is terrifying, but it is also astonishingly delightful. Throwing aside our fears leaves us absolutely exposed and defenseless, but at the first sign from the other that he is attracted by us in our exposed condition we begin to feel the same delight in ourself that he seems to feel and at the same time we delight in him. In friendship we say, "You and I both love me and you and I both love you." Hence surrender is not merely a road to conquest, it is not merely an instant of awesome terror, it is also the opening to ecstasy. Surrender is of the essence of the friendship promise, a friendship representing a beginning of the end of terror and a beginning of the beginning of delight. Friendship would be no challenge if it were not for the terror, but it would not be worth the risk if it were not for the delight. He who avoids the risk avoids the delight. He who is willing to run the risk finds that the delight far exceeds the terror.

Friendship, then, is an invitation to ecstasy, the gift of oneself, the promise that delight need never end in the playground that we and our friend can create together. Only a wise man attempts friendship, but only a foolish one refuses to attempt it. Alas for the poor creature man. There is no middle ground between wisdom and folly.

2

FRIENDSHIP AND LOVE

In the beginning of this book I assured the reader that I was neither a poet nor a philosopher nor a mystic but a social scientist, and yet, the rhetoric in the previous chapter, using as it did words like "surrender" and "ecstasy," were more from the lexicon of the mystic than that of the sociologist. However, man has no other words with which he can talk meaningfully about friendship. The vocabulary of romantic love may have connotations that makes serious discussion of friendship difficult. On the other hand, the vocabulary of romantic love has at least this advantage: Friendship *is* love.

There are many writers who would like to distinguish between friendship and love. Some would have us believe, for example, that love marks the beginning of marriage and friendship and declines during its later years. And yet others would argue that romantic love cannot survive very long into the marriage relationship. My own view, however, is that these distinctions are based on very narrow definitions of both love and friendship and very unjustified pessimism about the marriage relationship.

Love and friendship are the same thing. In the Christian tradition there is no doubt about this. "By this shall all men know that you are my disciples that you have love for one another. As I have loved you, so you love one another." And "behold, I do not call you servants, I call you friends."

It is frequently assumed that love is what man feels for his mate or for the person who is substituting for his mate and that friendship is an emotion that he feels for someone with whom he is not sleeping. But such an assumption is based on pre-Freudian notions of sexuality, since it supposes that love is sexual and friendship is not. As I have argued elsewhere, all human friendship has profoundly sexual over-tones, and marriage just happens to be that sexual relation-ship that provides a context for sexual intercourse.

There are a number of conclusions that follow:

Marriage is a friendship. If it is not a friendship, then it is not a satisfactory human relationship. And if it is not a satisfactory human relationship, the payoff in sexual inter-course between husband and wife is bound to be considerably less than satisfactory. Or, to put the matter more dramati-cally, sleeping with a member of the opposite sex is fully pleasurable only when one is sleeping with a friend. If the powerful physical urges of courtship and early marriage are not sustained by a developing friendship between husband and wife, then they rapidly decline both in power and in pay-off.

The marriage relationship is therefore the primordial human friendship. The surrender of man and woman to each other in intercourse is a symbol of their friendship and a powerful reinforcement of that friendship. It is possible to look at the marriage relationship as a laboratory for a study of the dynamics of friendship. It is not the only kind of friendship nor the only kind of sexual relationship (since all intimate friendships are sexual), but it is that sexual relationship where both the terror and the ecstasy are most obvious and most explicit. In this book, therefore, we will frequently use the marriage relationship to illustrate our reflections about friendship. The only vocabulary we have that enables us to discuss friendship adequately is the vocabulary that was developed to describe romantic love, a love that we are arguing can only survive in marriage if we happen to be married to a friend.

Sex without friendship, that is to say, sex without the kind of love that we are discussing in this volume, is at best unsatisfactory, and at worst, inhuman. Intercourse between two people who are not friends is a sham, since they are "making love" where in fact there is no love. From a psychodynamic viewpoint, a man who enters into the body of a wife who is not his friend is doing the same thing as if he were sleeping with a prostitute. In both instances the sexual act does not symbolize the promise, the gift, and the invitation that are the essence of friendship. Similarly, a wife who yields to or seduces a husband whom she despises is little different from a prostitute; both are pretending a conquest and a surrender that does not exist.

One ought not to conclude, of course, from such an observation that it makes no difference whether one sleeps with one's mate or with a prostitute. It makes all the difference in the world, even though psychodynamically the act may be the same. When one has made a public and presumably permanent commitment to one's mate, if there is not friendship in the relationship, it does not follow that one should seek out a prostitute, but rather it follows that one should attempt to determine why the mate is not a playmate and what has one contributed oneself to the failure of the friendship to survive or grow in the marriage.

Love and friendship then are the same thing—the open, trusting commitment of oneself to another human being. Since one always gives the whole of one's self in such a gift, including one's body, all friendship is sexual. The special kind of sexuality in a marriage relationship (which is the model and the root of all human friendship) can only be fully human and fully pleasurable when it exists in a context of friendship. Marriage does not destroy love; it requires it and becomes meaningless in its absence. If romantic love declines as the marriage years lengthen, it is because friendship has not developed. Husband and wife learn, as do all friends, how difficult and demanding the friendship relationship is. Any illusions they had during courtship that it would be easy are stripped away, but in a good married friendship the very difficulties and strains of the mutual surrender and conquest enhance the joy and pleasure of the union. It was suggested in the Introduction that friendship was like mountain climbing or professional football playing. That is to say, it was an activity the very difficulties of which increase the pleasure. In the context of evolving friendship, the difficulties of marriage make the romantic love of husband and wife stronger rather than weaker. In the absence of such friendship, difficulties dominate the scene, and the passion of the early years grows cold. But if passion grows cold, it is because the married lovers do not have the courage and the playfulness to be passionate friends.

We will use both the language of romantic lovers and the marriage relationship as an illustration in the rest of the book for marriage as the example *par excellence* of terror and delight of human friendship. It is also a classic illustration of how friendship is invitation, promise, and gift.

As a celibate, whose friendship experiences are of a different sort, it always seemed to me astonishing how much terror exists in marriage despite the fact that the husband

and wife have been living on very intimate terms both physically and psychologically. They may have been very successful at adjusting to the terror and at developing an elaborate series of rituals, conventions, by-laws, and customs that enable them to hide their terrors from one another and from themselves—and from the world around. It is only when one stumbles behind the veil that cloaks the relationship or is invited there to help that one discovers the extent of the mutual terror and the elaborate noncommunication that has been created to preserve the balance of terror—so elaborate, in fact, that the husband and wife will do all in their power to conceal it even from themselves.

The celibate is also astonished to see how easy it is to get married. A man and woman may marry each other because they feel physical passion for each other, because society expects them to get married, because they think marriage will firmly establish their masculinity or femininity, because marriage will please their parents and make them acceptable members of middle-class society, or because they have nothing else to do but to get married. They can go through a courtship, even one of considerable duration, talk very calmly and rationally about the future, engage in socially approved or even socially disapproved intimacies, and still be perfect strangers to one another. They can go through the horrendous ritual of the wedding ceremony, risk their bodies in the trial of their first act of love making, adjust to each other's peculiarities and eccentricities, even give birth to children, share the same bathroom and the same television set, live in the same house and drive the same car, and still remain, in the radical sense of the word, strangers. The relationship can go on and on without either partner risking the slightest particle of his selfhood or exposing the smallest bit of his terror. Vast areas of their relationship, including its most intimate dimensions, are covered by an immense conspiracy of silence in which problems do not exist because they are defined out of existence. The relationship is not very satisfactory but not so terribly unsatisfactory that it will fall apart. They do not ever see terror in one another's eyes nor do they see much delight either. They exist and they coexist, and questions of terror or delight are scarcely relevant. What might have been a friendship is now merely mutual accommodation.

But an accommodating relationship where two people who occasionally enjoy limited amounts of socially approved passion with one another is merely an exaggeration of most human relationships; the terror and delight of friendship are quickly snuffed out in nonmarital relationships, too, with the only important differences being that disillusionment is less severe because society has not yet progressed to a state where most of its members expect emotional payoffs in nonmarital relationships.*

From the point of view, then, of the outsider who is temporarily inside the veil that hides a married relationship from the world around, the capacity of a man and woman to live together and share virtually no element of their authentic selves is astonishing. Terror and delight can be snuffed out by everyday routine, though these repressed urges later surface after the children have left home in the constant, nagging nastiness that characterizes so many old couples who have lost the systematic escapes from one another that

* The quest for meaningful communities among young people today may indicate that an increasing number of them do want emotionally rewarding relationships—that is to say, friendships—with those who are not their partners in the marriage bed. This widening search for friendship is one of the great challenges and also one of the great risks of our time for, if a considerable proportion of marriage relationships end up as unsatisfying, one must assume that there are many strong barriers to mature and emotionally rewarding relationships that are not reinforced by payoff of genital sexuality.

37

child-rearing provided. We need only listen to husbands and wives on European vacations together to realize how much resentment a lifetime from hiding from one another has produced.

Though it is possible to hide from them, terror and delight may occasionally slip out, particularly under the influence of John Barleycorn—or, in a more recent era, perhaps under the influence of narcotics. Terror and delight are remembered on the morning after with chagrin and embarrassment. Rarely do the couple try to break through the fog of cigarettes, coffee, and hangover even to maintain the momentary hint of something better between them, much less to discuss the possibility that the moments might be lengthened.

Yet it is more difficult for husband and wife to hide from each other than to be open to one another; much effort and energy are required to keep up the pretense. A life of trust would probably be much more relaxing, however great its difficulties, than a life of constantly scurrying for cover. We human beings are quite practiced at hiding from one another. The race has had millions of years to develop skills, and we have had our whole lifetimes to integrate these skills into our own personality; coming out of our hiding would bring us much farther from the edge of the forest than the race is presently inclined to go.

And yet, when we stop to think about the matter objectively, it is an astonishing phenomenon. The overpowering attractiveness of a human body of the opposite sex and the intense challenge presented by such a body to the ultimate resources of our personality ought to keep married lovers in an almost constant anguished terror and delight; and the variegated appeals of the other's body, one would think, would paralyze our defense mechanisms. Our awareness of the compelling fascination that the other is able to exercise upon us ought to shake us to the very roots of our being; the calculating and intrigued appraisal of us in which the other is engaging ought to capture us in a fear that delights and that is fearsome. Or, to put the matter even more graphically, when a man and woman who are attracted to one another stand naked in each other's presence, every fiber of their body and spirit, every dimension of their personality are straining toward the expression of both terror and delight. That they are able to resist such impulses is a compliment, one supposes, to their ability to develop defense mechanisms, but not to their intelligence, nor their wit, nor their basic humanity.

The proportions of terror and delight obviously vary from time to time and couple to couple, but the point is that if a genital relationship is to remain healthy both of these elements must be preserved. That they are not preserved is merely evidence that the more awesome terror, the more ecstatic delight of psychological nakedness—that is to say, of friendship—has also been repressed. It takes great skill for two beings whose whole humanity—body and soul—is oriented toward union to be able to overcome the urge for union, but it is clear enough that a very large proportion of married couples are able to avoid union at every level of their mutual relationship. One must be impressed with their skills.

So they have invited one another to a life of incredible intimacy. They have given to each other their bodies in the fullest possible way and, by this gift, they have promised to one another a total openness to delight and to growth together. But the invitation lacked understanding, the gift was shallow, and the promise really was not serious. They discovered very shortly after their marriage that friendship, even friendship when reinforced by the ecstatic pleasures of genital union, demanded too much of themselves. The only alternative was to cool it psychologically and physically. The depth of human fear is obviously very great if it is able to cool such elementary and fiery human passions.

3

FRIENDSHIP AND SELF-REVELATION

The social psychologist, George Herbert Mead, writes of the "looking glass self." Without trying to analyze the complexity of Mead's thought in any great detail, one can say that the basic insight of Mead's psychology is that we perceive who we are by seeing ourself reflected in the reactions of others. The "looking glass self" is something more than just a passive image for the reflection we perceive, or permit ourselves to perceive on the faces of others; it not only tells us who we are but also determines what we will become. For a child, the approving reaction of the parent reinforces certain kinds of behavior, and his disapproval sanctions other kinds of behavior. The child learns that he is valuable when he makes mother smile and not valuable when she frowns. His personality is shaped, therefore, by the reaction of his parents in the very profound sense that it is from their reactions that he learns how to define what is good in him. In those happy circumstances where there is powerful reinforcement for the variety and integrity of the child's emerging personality, the

41

adult that the child becomes will have enough confidence in himself both to reveal himself to others and to accept the totality of their reaction to him. But most of us, in the present stage of the evolution of the race, enter adulthood with a narrow and constricted notion of our self-esteem and rather little confidence in the matter of revealing ourself to others. Furthermore, we become quite skillful at overlooking strong and positive reactions to those aspects of our personality for which we got negative reactions from our parent.

A neat example of this misperceiving of positive reactions is to be found in a very large number of beautiful women who sincerely and pervasively believe that they are not attractive despite overwhelming evidence to the contrary. In most instances, these women were perceived in childhood by their mothers as a rival and a threat; unconsciously but powerfully, the mother imposed sanctions on the child's attractiveness. To be attractive meant that one was to be punished, to be rejected, to be despised; therefore the little girl built a mechanism into her personality to shut out all evidence that suggested that she was attractive. If she was attractive she was bad, and if she was unattractive she was good. In adult life, then, the admiration of lovers and of her husband, the frank enjoyment of her beauty by other men and the equally frank envy of other women, are simply not strong enough to overcome her basic fear of being punished because she is attractive. She is not merely quite incapable of revealing herself to others but is terrified of a positive reaction to a self-revelation that might enhance her beauty.

She may become frigid or a nymphomaniac or a nagging bitch or a compulsive housewife, or any combination of these. To be a compulsive housewife, for example, waging constant war—generally unsuccessful—against the chaos created by her children is, in her personality experience, valid and approved feminine behavior. She was never punished for this. But to be an attractive woman is something that carries immense risks. Childhood experiences have maimed her self-esteem and have inhibited her from seeing signs that might begin to restore that self-esteem. If her husband can combine gentleness with persistence and firmness, if he can provide her with the constant warmth and support she needs while resolutely refusing to accept her cop-outs, she may begin to be infected by his belief in her attractiveness. The process will be a slow and difficult one.

One could rewrite the above description, making the appropriate changes in the genders in the nouns and pronouns, and say exactly the same thing about many males. They are afraid to accept their own masculinity precisely because that would make them a rival to their father, and their father did not tolerate rivals.

However badly damaged the mirror may be, it is still through the looking glass self that we grow. Those hidden talents and those secret aspirations, those repressed nobilities and those splendid dreams only can become real when we are able to show them to someone else whose positive response will assure us that our dreams, our hopes, our instincts are not only valid, but the most valid part of us. Similarly, our hidden fears and terrors must be brought out into the open so that someone else can dismiss them as foolishness. We grow as human beings by revealing ourselves to others and accepting their positive encouragement in return. The more they seem to approve that in us that most frightens us, the more confident we become in our self-revelation. With each new unveiling of the self we, of course, are afraid that they will laugh or ridicule or turn away in disgust. They cannot possibly like us when they know us as we *really are,* but, wonder of wonders, they apparently do.

Self-revelation, then, is an unveiling, a kind of psychological striptease, which is totally different, one must note,

43

than exhibitionism, for the exhibitionist displays himself indiscriminately and crudely. He is actually trying to hide himself under a pretense of phony openness (about which more in a later chapter). Self-display is a slow, steady process in which one move grows naturally from the previous move. It cannot be hurried, it cannot be forced, it cannot be done in one spectacular display. It is painful and pleasurable and terrifying and delightful. We simply cannot believe that the other really likes us. We are afraid that he does not, and then we are caught in an even worse fear that he does because, if he does, then he is going to demand still more of us; his demand to possess us fully will never stop.

Self-revelation is both the indispensable core of personality expansion and the essential gift-giving of friendship. We become fuller, richer, warmer, more humane human beings, precisely to the extent that we are able to enter into friendship relationships. The more we permit the lover to know us, the more worthy of his love we become; as his searching gaze probes ever deeper into our personality, he discovers riches of which no one else was ever aware and in which we scarcely dare to believe. But, because he sees within us, we actually become the good that he sees. By reinforcing the very tentative inclinations of the beloved, the lover actually creates his beloved. We become that which the lover wants us to be, and he becomes that which we want him to be. When he reacts positively to our tentative, fragile, yet courageous self-revelation, with warmth and affection and encouragement, we discover resources in ourselves of which we had always dreamed but whose reality we could not believe. The lover, in other words, is a person who makes our dreams about ourselves come true.

Self-revelation, then, is the tension between terror and delight. It is a conflict between the desire to hide and to hold back and the desire to communicate and to be open.

We are afraid of making a spectacle of ourselves and, yet, there is a secret inclination to try, a thin little hope that if we do so the lover will consider our spectacle not folly but beauty. We are terribly ambivalent about the reaction. It would be devastating if he thought us ugly, but even more devastating if he thought us beautiful; then we would have to be beautiful for him all the time, and indeed, more beautiful as time went on. That would be a demand with which we could not possibly be comfortable.

Self-revelation is a big risk; the other may reject us, he may ridicule us, he may not be strong enough to cope with our self-revelation no matter how tentative it may originally be. He may have too much investment in preserving the systematic defenses that keep the two of us apart. He may retreat behind the barrier of misunderstanding us, of refusing to listen beyond our words, especially when the words come choked with anger, as words of self-revelation frequently do. He may understand that we are attempting to seduce him, that if he listens to our self-revelation, if he is willing to give himself over to delight in our most private self, then he will have to reveal himself in response; such a thought may be a terror too awful to bear. He may choose not to believe us or to believe himself, or he may accept our self-revelation for a while and then turn on us when he feels himself being drawn too close to us. He may be clinical, objective, detached, and faintly amused at first, but when he sees himself being drawn into a relationship that is intricate, complex, and profound, he may panic and scurry away from us in terror, perhaps leaving behind a defense mechanism of fear, hatred, and anger to keep us from pursuing him. It is as though on the wedding night the bride's revelation of her body was greeted with laughter or contempt or by her husband's fleeing the room in terror. The damage that such behavior would do to her personality might be very great. Similarly,

45

the damage that can be done by a rejection of the offer of one's self in friendship can be devastating. Even those who are strong enough to take such punishment are going to be wary the next time they try.

But there's no point in minimizing the risks of rejection. Life is, unfortunately, not like a Hollywood movie in that every human relationship has a reasonably happy ending. Some human relationships, perhaps even most human relationships, are tragic or at least frustrating. Friendships can be undertaken with enthusiasm and joy only to terminate in bitterness and disappointment. Only the most naïve can sail serenely into a friendship without any thought of the dangers involved. And even the naïve would probably not make that mistake twice.

It does no good, therefore, to romanticize the issues involved in friendship. One can hurt, one frequently will get hurt in attempting friendship. The risk is real, and it never goes away.

It is precisely the risk involved that makes people hold back, and it is precisely the initial resistance to the invitation of friendship that destroys so many possibilities for friendship. Especially in the marriage relationship, the barriers of shame and nagging and petty conflict are almost ready to collapse when the two lovers turn away from one another. They have been able to risk themselves up to the point where they are almost successful and then, at the last moment, as though they realize the implications of a little more persistence, they turn away from the relationship and settle for coexistence rather than friendship.

On occasion we persist in friendship and attempts at friendship long after it has become obvious that the risks were a mistake and that one has been rejected; but by far the more common error is to quit just before friendship actually begins. We snatch defeat from the jaws of victory.

There comes a time in a relationship between friends when the risks of self-revelation have become minimal, when one can, for all practical purposes, be certain that the mutual giving in a friendship relationship will not stop. The turning point has been reached, and the friends will be friends forever. It takes a long time for a relationship to develop to this state, and those who prematurely announce that their commitment to one another is definitive and irrevocable are only deceiving themselves. However sure one is that the exchange of gifts is irrevocable, there still remains not only the residue of terror but also the necessity for a redefinition of the relationship as the two friends change and grow. When a friendship has become irrevocable, the demands it makes on the friendship partners are not lessened, but the friends are able to be confident that they have passed the point of no return.

Self-revelation requires tact, patience, sensitivity, receptiveness to the other's self-revelations, persistence, and firmness. The pace of self-revelation, as we have said, cannot be accelerated or hurried or pushed. We must not push either ourself or the other. On the other hand, we cannot tolerate in the other a deceleration of the process, and we must plead with him not to tolerate it in us. It is not a game in which one move must be matched by another move but, rather, two complex games that interweave with one another and move at different speeds. The two friends adjust as two dancers in an intricate dance pattern; invitation, gift, promise, conquest, surrender—all must be blended into the pattern of one's own self-revelation while one simultaneously adjusts to meet the past, present, and anticipated future moves of one's partner in the pattern. The pace of the dance is sometimes so breathtaking that one feels like it is time to withdraw to catch one's breath, and at other times it is so maddeningly slow that one wishes the music would stop.

47

The paradox of the dance of friendship is that neither partner can assume total responsibility for its success, and yet both must hold themselves totally responsible for what happens.

The ultimate requirement for success in the dance is that the dancer have at least some initial confidence in his abilities as a dancer. He thus does not need to have his patterns validated by initial response from the partner. He can afford to risk himself because he knows that there is something there in himself, even if the partner will not respond to it. He can persist in his offer of friendship long after the weak man would be forced to retreat in anger and hurt; but he is also strong enough to be able to end the dance when it is clear the partner is simply unwilling or unable to dance. The weak man terminates the dance much too soon because he is afraid that he will be completely destroyed by rejection or continue it much too long because, if the dance should end, there would be nothing of himself left.

Friendship is only for those who believe that they do have something worth revealing to a friend, that there is an intrinsic value in them which others ought to find attractive. The trouble with most human friendships is that one, or usually both, of the partners really are not convinced that they have anything to offer.

4

FRIENDSHIP AND SHAME

The root of the problem is our own feeling of inadequacy, that is to say, our shame. The terror that stands as a barrier to friendship is clothed in shame. The delight that comes from acting in the face of the terror is a delight in the overcoming of shame.

Shame tells us that we are not good enough, that we cannot stand the test of being seen for what we are, that if we are exposed we will be seen as inadequate. Adam and Eve's shame in the Garden of Eden came precisely when they were exposed not as man and woman, for they already knew they were man and woman, but rather as failures who did not honor a commandment given them.

Man is the only animal capable of shame, the only one to whom it would occur that he might be inadequate, the only for whom there exists the possibility that others, when they see him as he is, will ridicule him and declare him to be valueless and worthless. Chimpanzees are very high in self-esteem.

Shame is the fear of physical inadequacy, indeed, of sexual inadequacy. A man is not sure he is enough of a man to be able to cope with his woman, and the woman is not certain that she is enough of a woman to be able to respond to her man. Sexual inadequacy is more than just genital inadequacy, though genitality is certainly involved. It implies that a person is unable to do those things that a man does in his society or those things that a woman does.

To be a man means more than to be able to have an orgasm with a woman. It means that he must support his family in dignity and comfort, that he must achieve in the competitive world of occupation and career, that he must be thought of as a success, that he must be able to impress other males with his own masculinity, that he must be able to think of himself as aggressive, hard-driving, vigorous, determined, and competent. And to be a woman means more than just responding to man's sexual overtures. It means being a good housekeeper and mother and chauffeur and social organizer, creator of Halloween costumes, hostess at successful parties, and helpful wife of a man who is deemed to have made it in the competitive world. A man who has not achieved male success will feel very inadequate in the genital relationship. He will have to prove himself. His whole life will be a series of tests in which his masculinity is proven. Failure is likely to be pervasive no matter what his actual success is in the real world; if he is driven hard enough, there is no success, marital or occupational, that will give him enough validity. Similarly, for a woman, if her doubts about her femininity are powerful enough she will not be able to succeed in any of those dimensions of activity that are rated by society as establishing her womanhood or, even if she does succeed and succeed brilliantly, the success will not be enough to persuade her of her femininity.

A man who must prove his maleness and a woman who must prove her femaleness are bad risks for friends but, given the human propensity to seek out neurotic relationships, the two of them are very likely to marry one another.

The major problem with a person who feels that he is inadequate is that he confuses limitations with inadequacies. We are necessarily finite and limited beings; not all of us are destined to be college or corporation presidents—or cardinal archbishops, for that matter. But we have not made peace with ourselves. We interpret limitations, finite incompleteness, as indicating inadequacy. If we cannot do everything, then we are not worth anything. If we can't achieve eminence, then we are a failure. If we can't be something that we are not, and are held simply to be ourselves, then life is a disaster.

A good deal of the stress and the strain of the human condition come from our striving to be something that we are not and, in the course of the process, ignoring that which we are. We put in immense and compulsive efforts on our careers because we are convinced that since we are basically inferior, this is the only way we can catch up with and maintain an even pace with those who are our superiors.

Such compulsion, of course, is independent of reality. The graduate student who torments himself about the necessity of having a perfect doctoral dissertation is convinced that he is so inadequate as a student that only a perfect dissertation will win over the faculty barons from their organized conspiracy against him. One may assure such a student that the faculty's only interest is in giving him a degree and getting him the hell out of the department. He may even be told that he is one of the most promising and able students that the faculty has seen in a long time and that all he must do is finish the final chapter of his dissertation. But he knows better. The faculty is out to get him because they see through him, they are aware of his inferiority and inadequacy, that he must strive to perform far beyond his abilities lest he be found out. For the inadequate person, instant perfection is the only response to a threatening external world. To show the slightest limitation or finitude is to leave oneself open to the circling birds of prey. As years go on, the graduate student becomes more competitive, he must constantly watch his colleagues because, of course, they're all out to get him, all out to strip away his defenses and to reveal him for the fraud and the failure that he knows he is. He may be unaware of its existence, but it still dominates his life. One can imagine what kind of husband he will make.

The root of the graduate student's inadequacy is in his familial past. No matter what he did, he was never able to win the approval of his parents. He was inadequate to their demands; unless he can come to terms with this fact, he will be inadequate for the rest of his life. He will have to hide, he will not be able to give of himself because the initial gift that he offered to his parents was rejected. How can he believe he is attractive when he was not attractive to them?

The truth of the matter is that we are all attractive. There is no such thing, at least outside of the mental institutions, as a human personality that does not have the potential to attract other human personalities. Nor is there any such thing, outside of physical disaster, as an unattractive human body. The thought that one's body may be attractive is an appalling idea for many people, so appalling for some, in fact, that they engage in behavior that deprives the body of its attractiveness (of which overeating is the most obvious example). Human attractiveness is not really a matter of the arrangement of the features or the dimensions of various sections of the body. There is a certain physical perfection to be found especially in youth that can be over-whelmingly attractive, however shallow it may prove itself, but authentic human beauty results from a combination of the physical and the psychic, with both influencing each other. Glamor photographers have observed that after a certain age of life (they say twenty-five for most people) attractiveness becomes increasingly a dimension of the personality rather than of the body. In other words, whether we are beautiful or not depends to a very considerable extent on our own free choice.

That is a fairly horrendous thought. Not merely is the shape of our personality something within our control, but even our physical attractiveness. We are adequate or in-adequate, not because of the body with which we've been equipped, not even because of the past experiences we have had, but largely because of the choice we make, the choice between shame and self-respect. If we wish to believe that we are inadequate, then surely we will be inadequate both physi-cally and psychologically; but if there is even a small corner of our personality where there is a strong conviction of our adequacy, then shame will not stop us from being human be-ings whose attractiveness is irresistible.

One of the escapes we fashion from our own inadequacy is to set up standards that are not only impossible but inappropriate for who and what we are. An able, intelli-gent graduate student who would make a superb teacher at a good, small liberal arts college cannot accept such a berth because he has been trained to aspire to be a senior faculty member at a great research university. In his own judgment he must be worthless because he cannot live up to the false standards he has set for himself. Similarly, a woman concludes that she is deficient as a female because her breasts are not of the proportions usually to be observed on the "playmate of the month" and thus conveniently can escape the fact that her physical proportions are appropriate for *her* and, if they were any different, she would not be more of a woman but less one. Inadequacy and shame are not things that merely happen to us; they are, in the final analysis, things we choose.

But why would we be so stupid as to choose them? Inadequacy, it turns out, is very useful, and there are big advantages in shame. Shame and inadequacy are powerful excuses for not trying to break out of the barriers we build around ourselves. If we can maintain shame that is a powerful enough force we are excused from taking the risk of offering ourself in friendship. Shame justifies our frigidity; frigidity in turn reinforces our shame. We are not good enough to be friends; we will not try to be a friend to anyone; we will strongly resist attempts at friendship from anyone else. Furthermore, as we become more practiced in our frigidity, we develop methods of blaming it on others. We offer ourselves to others in such a way as to guarantee that they will reject us. Frigidity is not our fault but their fault. We want to be friends, but they will not have us because of their own meanness and ugliness. They turn us off; we couldn't even face the possibility that they turn us off because we want them to turn us off.

Psychological frigidity is closely connected to physical frigidity. The two are linked to each other, as body and spirit are apt to be linked, though one can be psychologically frigid and still go through the motions of not being physically frigid. The frigid personality is not capable of giving itself to another in openness and trust. Our fear of genital inadequacy is merely the focus for a larger fear of personal and human inadequacy. Shame is the fear that we are not good enough to obtain a response from another and surely not good enough to respond to others' invitations to us.

54

What indeed would happen if we were not frigid? What would happen to us if we permitted just a little bit of our personality to show? We might lose control. The rest of us might be forced to thaw and then we would be exposed, then we would be naked, then we would be seen as we are. Our inadequacy would be open to all; there would be no escape from the contemptuous gaze of others and from public ridicule.

Frigidity is generally thought of as a female problem, and physiologically it is probably more frequently an affliction of women than of men. The man is able to have an orgasm more easily than a woman, though psychological frigidity can easily coexist with orgasm. As a matter of fact, both the nymphomaniac and the Don Juan are humanly frigid; their genital activity is merely a defense mechanism for their gnawing doubts and fears. Both of them are children who were never able to grow up to be a man or a woman; no matter how many orgasms they have, they're still not sure of their sexuality. They are plagued by very grave doubts about their humanity, are convinced of their inadequacy, and are covered with shame.

The only way to overcome shame is to take risks, to expose ourselves to others, to support them, and to seduce them into supporting us. We see how erroneous our shame is when the adequacy that shame calls into question is strongly validated by the reactions of others to us. We must permit them to react, and then we must permit ourselves to see the reaction. We must permit ourselves to understand that they see us not as a collection or organs or personality traits or occupational skills or economic accomplishments but as a *person* whose worth and values transcend the shape of a body or the size of the checks sent each year to the Internal Revenue Service. The most decisive choice any of us will make in our lives hinges on the question of whether we are willing to begin to accept others' reaction to us, particularly those to whom we have tentatively entrusted enough of ourselves so that they may call themselves our friends. If we are willing to give our friends an opportunity to support us and if we are willing to risk ourselves in supporting our friends, then shame can be overcome. Shame inhibits risk-taking but can be conquered by risk-taking. Only if we are willing to believe that we have nothing to be ashamed of can our risk-taking become successful; but, on the other hand, unless we can begin to take risks we will never believe we have nothing to be ashamed of.

Shame has a strong bodily residence; it is rooted ultimately in feelings of sexual inadequacy, but creates a more generalized sense of personal inadequacy. Some contemporary psychologists, most of them of the pop psychology variety, have concluded that the solution to the problem is a direct attack on physical shame; touching, groping, pawing, kneading bodies of others and letting them do the same to us is taken to be a healthy progress against shame. This philosophy of "group probing" reached its height at a recent meeting of the World Council of Churches at Uppsala, Sweden, where one of the practitioners intoned to the assembled delegates, "Not let us pray, but let us touch." And the magazine *Psychology Today* published an article in which the most extravagant kinds of claims for success of nude encounter marathons were made.

One surely doesn't want to deny that those of us in the Anglo-Saxon tradition are badly hung up on physical contact. There could be a lot more touching and embracing in our lives than there is. Furthermore, there is probably more fear of nakedness—and obsession about it—in the Anglo-Saxon world than is either appropriate or healthy. But a mad enthusiasm for ripping off our clothes and pawing each other is no solution either to cultural difficulties or personal problems. For however much physical resonance there may be to our feelings of shame, in adult life these feelings have gone far beyond physical shame and now have a major impact in personal and human shame. We feel inadequate, not merely sexually, but as total human beings. Nude marathons and other such activities surely provide us with strong emotional jolts—as do marijuana and LSD—but there is no reason to think that such emotional jolts are particularly helpful in enabling us to deal with the complex and intricate relationship between physical and psychological shame that affects our personality. Nor is there the slightest justification for the extravagant claims that some psychologists make for such behavior.

Nude marathons may produce human beings who are skilled practitioners of exhibitionism and who run away from themselves and reality by exhibitionism, but there is no theoretical or empirical reason for thinking they can cure anything. They are a part of the purely American tendency to attempt to solve complicated issues with simple solutions, to achieve instantaneous results by jumping on the bandwagon of the latest fad rather than to put in the long, arduous hours of effort that are inevitably required for human growth. Intimacy of whatever sort is only possible among very close friends, and friendship takes a long time to develop. Instantaneous friendships on a weekend orgy scarcely are an appropriate context for intimacy. While there may be intimacy possible among friends that we have not yet explored in Western society, and while there might very well not be enough physical intimacy in relationships between most husbands and wives, it seems safe to say from what we know of the human personality that physical intimacy is more likely to flow from friendship than to produce it. As one astute psychologist has remarked, "If you have a neurotic take off his clothes, all you're going to have is a naked neurotic."

Shame, then, if it is to be overcome at all, will not be overcome by dramatic gestures but rather by careful, patient risk-taking and firm and insistent demands that our friend who has offered himself to us be also ready to take the risks. The friendship process is inevitably and necessarily a dualistic process. It is not enough that we take risks with ourself, we must also demand that the other take risks with himself. It is not enough that he encourage us to disclose ourself to him; he must also demand that we encourage him to disclose himself to us. He must require that we put aside our shame but, at the same time, he must require that we require him to put aside his shame. When one stops to think of the intricate patterns of the friendship relationship, one becomes perhaps a little less surprised that there are so few friends in the world.

5

FRIENDSHIP AND TRANSFERENCE

The means of avoiding friendship are multiple, but they are not random. We integrate them into specific psychodynamic techniques that enable us to keep others at bay and feel justified in doing so. The most dramatic and most effective and most pervasive defense against friendship is a process that psychoanalysts call transfer.

In psychoanalytic terminology, transference is the process by which we turn the therapist into a duplication of the parent whose relationship with us is at the root of our emotional problems. Although the transference phenomenon has a precise and technical meaning in psychoanalytic literature (at least reasonably precise, for psychoanalysts seem to have a hard time agreeing on definitions of anything), it also is merely a manifestation of a form of human behavior that is well nigh universal. The unresolved problems from our familial past intrude themselves, if we let them, into every human relationship we have. Rather than face the other as a potential friend we distort the other, we make him into someone he is not, we invest him with the characteristics that were a trial to us in our parent, and then we take out on him the repressed hatred and anger we feel toward that parent.

If we are good at transference distortion, and most of us are very good, we seek out as a partner in our relationship somebody who will be able to find in us precisely those characteristics that he has not been able to cope with in his own parents. In splendid neurotic fashion, we can expend all the energies of the relationship on fighting with surrogate parents and really ignore each other. Often when one observes a husband and wife constantly at each other's throats, one is forced to conclude that what is happening is that the husband's mother and the wife's father are fighting with each other and using their children merely as pawns.

Childhood is necessarily our first experience with intimacy, an experience which for many of us is far less than satisfactory. But we learn, as we struggle through the childhood years, certain basic methods of coping with the problems of intimacy. These methods may involve openness to other human beings but more likely will involve sophisticated ways of escaping from them. When we are faced with intimacy in adult life we fall back on the behavior models of our childhood. If these models are less than open and trusting, we throw up hasty barriers to fend off those who want to become close to us, barriers that were designed to cope with our parents or our siblings and that necessitate converting the potential friend into a substitute for a parent or a sibling.

This process of converting and distorting the other is a very subtle one. When we pause to consider it objectively, we realize how fantastically clever the human unconscious is. First of all, we seek out as friends those who remind us of our parents, which in itself is not necessarily a problem, since we find in such friends some of the same qualities that made our parents attractive. But we are also likely to find qualities similar enough to those things that we feared and hated in our parents to justify our fearing and hating our friends. Then we selectively perceive the behavior of the friend so it may fit our unconscious paradigm of the parent or sibling. In other words, those things that the friend does that make him most like our parent we emphasize, and those things that make him very distinct from our parent we ignore. Finally, and this is the most sophisticated aspect of all, our unconscious seeks out the weak links in the friend's personality; it probes, pries, twists, pushes to determine what kinds of pressures from us will make him behave neurotically toward us. What aspects of his personality, in other words, can be twisted not merely so that he may be interpreted as a parent but so that he may behave in ways similar to the way our parents behaved toward us. We seduce him, in other words, not into being the best in himself but into being the worst of himself. We enlist his collaboration in distorting his personality, and he may be doing the same to us. We pressure him into a situation in which that which is most neurotic in him becomes dominant. In order that we may deal with him in some kind of relationship of pseudointimacy, we force him to partially destroy the best that is in himself.

The practice is admittedly diabolic. After one has been caught in it, one is astonished at how subtle and effective it is. Two human beings who choose to come together in intimacy or who are forced together in intimacy will either disclose themselves to one another or they will collaborate in a mutual process of distortion. Between self-revelation and distortion there seems to be no middle ground.

Paradoxically, the same friendship partners can go in either direction. There are marriage relationships in which

the husband and wife could be skillful in bringing out either
the best or the worst in each other. They frequently choose
to bring out the worst, although they are, in the early years of
marriage, only a hair's breadth from bringing out the best. A
man, for example, may be terribly insecure about his masculinity, and yet with the slightest show of encouragement from his
wife rapidly grow in confidence about his maleness; his wife,
in her turn, may be deeply troubled about her adequacy as a
woman, and yet be on the verge of breaking out of those troubles with the slightest reinforcement from her husband. Thus if
the man insistently and gently argues that she is a beautiful
woman, treats her as such, and demands that she behave as
such, she will become what he believes she is. If she encourages
and exhalts and enjoys her husband's maleness, then he will
quickly become that which she enjoys. But if she nags him,
pushes him, and resists his timid, awkward overtures, then
she will destroy his masculinity. If he allows himself to be
put off by her bitching and frigidity, then she will become
convinced that she is in fact nothing more than a frigid
bitch. The balance between the two of them is delicately set.
They usually manage to stay just slightly out of phase with
one another, with the husband attempting friendship when
the wife is afraid of it and the wife making overtures when
the husband is fearful. If ever through some slight miscalcu-
lation they should both take the initiative to turn their dance
of fear into a dance of trust, they might be unable to turn
back. They are both quite careful not to do this.

The dance of fear, it is to be supposed, is usually an
unconscious one; yet if one probes a little one discovers that
it is not completely unconscious, that there are many women
who know deep down what kind of support their husbands
need to feel confident of their manhood. They can be persuaded, if caught unawares, to say quite explicitly how
they ought to behave if they want to build up their husband's

ego. Yet they quickly suppress this information. If their husband is permitted to become confident of his masculinity, then it will be much harder to distort who and what he is. To allow him to plug up the chinks in his armor would be to weaken the whole transference neurosis in their relationship. The wife is quite sure she doesn't want to risk this.

Similarly, most men are not as grossly stupid as the way they treat their wives would suggest; but to modify the relationship so as to strengthen her confidence in her womanhood would be to risk far more of themselves than husbands are willing to risk. The man and woman could each help each other to become fully male and fully female, but that would necessitate abandoning the distortion of both their personalities on which they have systematically embarked. There is too much invested in the distortion to give it up.

The outside observer may ponder what ecstasies and what delights it would be to help a woman to gain more confidence in her feminine strength and attractiveness; but he can't understand how her husband persists in acting toward her with a combination of petty complaints and cold indifference. He would like to think that if he were in the husband's position he would be such a combination of firmness and warmth that the woman would come alive and blossom. But it is easy for the outside observer to say this. It is easy for him to forget that the complaints and the indifference really hide timidity. It is easy for him to overlook the fact that if he were in the same position his own insecure masculinity would be every bit as much in jeopardy as the woman's husband's. Ecstasy of delight there may be in feminizing her but also great terror.

Distortion of our friend then is not altogether unconscious or unintended. It becomes a more insistent and vigorous distortion precisely to the extent that we and the other come closest to breaking out of the barriers of fear in which we are caught. There is no need to engage in mutual distortion if we are at a distance from one another or if there is little hope that we can liberate each other from fear or shame. We fall back on the residues of our unresolved conflict with our parents only when it becomes necessary to guarantee that someone would not get close to us, so close he may be able to see through the heavy veils in which we have enshrouded ourselves.

The essence of the transference neurosis is the construction of a tightly interlocking network of hurts, injuries, and angers. Our unconscious can be persuaded that the friend is indeed the parent or sibling reincarnate if we are able to draw up a long indictment containing all the offenses the other has committed against us. It is well to note these offenses in great detail and to keep them constantly in mind, because if we should become slovenly about tallying the injuries that we have endured, we may some day just possibly see the other for who he really is and not for the surrogate parent or sibling that we've made him. If that happens, then it may be necessary for the encounter between the two of us to become authentic instead of distorted. Every effort must be bent to keep the distortion from being recognized as such and to thereby avoid authenticity. Should authenticity intrude itself we would be forced to acknowledge our fears and our shame and to risk ourselves with the other person. We would have to be what we both are and not the father figure or mother figure or brother figure or sister figure that we have succeeded in becoming for each other.

The transference defense mechanism is extraordinarily vicious. It ignores the warmth and the goodness about the other, ignores who and what he really is. It fastens on the weak points and the deficiencies of his personality and blows them up to the total personality. By defining him as

64

someone he is not, we actually push him down the road to becoming not the best in himself but the worst in himself. Our own neurosis becomes a joint chain with his neurosis to tie him to the ground. We not only take offense where he intended no offense, but we also force him into offending us when, if he could be himself, he really would not want to do so. It is not merely that our fear and our shame and our timidity destroy ourself, it is also necessary that we destroy the other unless somehow in a weak moment we permit him to liberate us from terror. Not only is our own happiness to be destroyed, but so is his. And of course we will enthusiastically cooperate with him while he helps us to destroy our own happiness.

How does one escape from the distortion of authenticity involved in a transference neurosis? The first step is the acknowledgment of the possibility that such a distortion may exist. Curiously enough, this acknowledgment is the most difficult step of all. Even psychologically sophisticated people find it very difficult to admit that they have an unconscious and that their unconscious is exercising powerful and perhaps controlling influence on their behavior. Other people may convert spouses or friends into surrogate siblings and parents, but we would never do a thing like that. The problems we have are not emotional problems, they are all rational, and we have nothing to do with them. They have been caused by the other. If he will only admit his guilt and modify his behavior, then there will be no difficulty in our friendship growing.

But, in fact, it is safe to assume that in any intimate human relationship that is not able to progress down the path to friendship the responsibility is mutual. Only when each partner can frankly acknowledge the possibility that he may have considerable unconscious emotional investment in maintaining the inauthenticity of the relationship will progress begin. Only if we can concentrate on what we have contributed to the quarrel is there any hope for resolution, but to begin an analysis of our own contribution and the possible unconscious roots of it is to begin a process from which there may be no escape and no return. Better that we do not try it.

We also should be aware that at those precise times that we are most likely to feel fury toward our partner we are quite likely in a situation where the systematic barriers we created around ourselves are most seriously threatened. The partner makes us most angry when he seems to be attacking that in our personality of which we are most ashamed. If at such a moment we stop listening to his words and listen to what he is really saying, then it may turn out that he is in fact trying to communicate to us that our fears are baseless and that he wants to love us if only we would give him a chance. He may not be brave enough to say such a thing quite so explicitly but at the very time there is the most anger in our relationship it is very likely that is precisely what one dimension of his personality is desperately trying to say.

So fear generates fear; distrust generates distrust; distortion generates distortion. And openness, however slight, can generate more openness; trust, however weak, can generate more trust; and confidence in one's own value, however thin, can generate more confidence in both us and the other. Whether we like it or not, a friend has been entrusted to us. Transference hedges our invitation to him, takes back our gift, and violates our promise. It distorts him and, instead of helping him be more than he is, it makes him much less than he is. It exploits his timidity, his shame, his terror. It offers him no opportunity for delight. We do not expose ourself to the other and seduce him into exposing himself to us. Transference is the last set of bars in the prison, bars that grow all the more strong when we begin to look outside the prison and see what the world beyond the bars could really be like.

6

LOSING IN THE FRIENDSHIP GAME

One of the most pathetic sights on the television screen is
an athletic team that has lost its desire to win. It may be
a game in which they are so badly behind their opponents
that there is no point in further effort, or it may be a
whole season, or it may be the end of the season when the
pressure is on; but, under whatever circumstances, a team
that has no desire to win is a grotesque caricature of itself.
It stumbles through the motions, makes disastrous mistakes,
loses its self-confidence, and, finally, seems to be bent upon
doing everything it can to hand victory on a silver platter
to the other side.

The athletic team that seeks its own self-destruction is
an excellent symbol of those human beings who do all that
they can to lose in the friendship game. The team that has
lost confidence in itself hates its coach or manager or owner
and wants to prove its utter worthlessness and, at the same
time, punish all those who are responsible for the worth-

lessness—front office, fans, or journalists. The loser in the friendship game who has no faith in himself seeks to punish those who proclaim they love him and eagerly courts his own destruction, all the time blaming others for it.

No one is a born loser, but some people have had childhood experiences that are such that they are losers for all their lives. They have immense talents, great promise, marvelous charm, impressive potential, but they always lose. Their marriages are not happy, their friendships are shallow, their careers obscure, their productivity minor or nonexistent. They spin great dreams about what they are going to do someday—particularly when under the influence of John Barleycorn—but the reality of their lives is dull, monotonous mediocrity.

They lose because they want to lose. Deep in the unconscious recesses of their personalities are powerful needs for failure and for hatred of those who tell them that failure is unnecessary. They *know* quite the contrary. *Failure* is absolutely essential. Unless they fail they will not be able to survive.

But why is it so important to be a loser? What are the payoffs in self-defeat?

First of all, by defeating ourselves we punish those toward whom we feel aggressive. Does someone count on us? Is there anyone who wants us to succeed? Have we made a commitment to another person? Splendid! We can convert that person into a substitute parent and then punish him for having the gall to expect anything from us.

As Samuel J. Warner puts it in his *Self-Realization and Self-Defeat,* "Self-defeat is a technique for achieving a sense of power, where there *is* real power 'for' partial or complete self-destruction: power to thwart and annoy the employer or teacher; power to disappoint or break the hearts of those who depend upon one's success; power to defy the fates and the forces of the universe. In this self-engineered failure or in suicide one *is* master of one's fate."*

Furthermore, failure is a successful defense against anxiety. If success is a real possibility, the anxiety feelings may become very high. We don't deserve success; we're not good enough. Besides, someone is likely to try to take it away from us just when it is within our grasp, so let's not try, let's cool it, let's limit the risk-taking. Better not to try at all than to try and fail.

If we do let ourselves go, if we do try our best, if we do make a serious commitment, we run the risk of being exposed for what we really are, we may be, heaven save us, criticized. There may be retaliation from the competitive and hostile forces around us. If we succeed, there is certainly going to be someone who will try to punish us, but we are too clever to let that happen. We will punish and frustrate our enemies by failing; then they can't do anything to us.

The loser must be a hater. He has to blame someone for his losses. He must prove that some authority figure is an evil genius behind his latest failure. Indeed, the injustice of the authority figure (whoever it happens to be at a given time) is an obsession with the loser. If anyone gives him half a chance he will spend hours glorifying in the offenses of the unfortunate person who happens to be his supervisor.

But he also has a way of getting even with that parent-monster: by withholding quality performance he is able to exercise power over him, by making him wait to the last minute he is able to display his independence, by failing he may even be able to make the authority figure look bad to others—oh, ecstasy of ecstasies!

Finally, the loser can maintain his pride and self-respect

* Samuel J. Warner, *Self-Realization and Self-Defeat*. New York: Grove Press, 1968, p. 93.

by being a perfectionist. Since there are so many enemies waiting to pounce on him he must—like Avis—try harder. He cannot let go of a project until it is absolutely perfect. Thus he is able to justify delays, procrastination, and shoddy, fourth-rate work. If he only had more time he would have done it perfectly but, as it is, the unfair time limitation imposed by a hostile world forces him to produce something that is so far beneath his own high standards that he can disavow all responsibilities for it.

Warner comments on a remark of a self-defeatist, " 'I seem to want to have the feeling that I'm best in *everything,* and if I'm not best in everything then I'm nothing.' It is consequently not difficult to grasp the meaning of this man's need to procrastinate. He fears putting himself to the test of action, for he would find his performance to be less than perfect, and this would rearouse dreaded underlying feelings of worthlessness and insignificance."[†]

The loser is a pathetic creature. If only he could put as much energy into life as he does into excuses, he might be a great man.

But my sympathy for him is limited by the fact that he is also a vengeful, punitive, and destructive person. He cannot abide the success of others. He hates those whose achievements are rightfully his. He's a superb critic, marvelously skilled at destroying others without ever running risks for himself. He is a great armchair prophet, a cocktail party theologian who talks big about what he is going to do, but he never does it. He's far too busy cutting others to pieces; the ones most likely to suffer his ire are precisely those who are most eager to love him, most ready to support his most authentic self and his real talent.

Warner sums up the fears of the self-defeating person:

[†] *Ibid.,* p. 71.

"Such a person feels fears in being spontaneous. He cannot expose the products of selfhood to the eyes of others, and since novelty is essential to creative unfolding of the self's possibilities, he represses the inner richness of his being, and embraces instead only those areas of his inner life which readily fit the socially 'safe' cliché. Here, the urge toward self-realization falls prey to the untoward need for acceptance by significant figures of the social scene . . . he fears his own impulses and fears knowing himself . . . he fears as well truly communicating with others lest this reveal what is actually going on within himself."‡

Of course, the loser was badly injured in childhood. The fear and suspicion that are part of the human condition have become so pathological in him that the only defense left to him against those who threaten him is his own gradual self-destruction. Losing is the ultimate in defense mechanisms. We say to the other, "Rather than let you have me, I will destroy myself first. Rather than running the risk of responding to your affection, I will degrade myself and thus punish you. You are, after all, nothing more than the reincarnation of my parent who hated me, and by punishing myself I punish you and that parent. I may be worthless, but you have made me worthless, and we shall both suffer together for my worthlessness."

The loser is very clever at arranging martyrdom situations. He writes the scenarios for his little dramas in such a way that he is made to look like an innocent victim and the other like a guilty monster, and then he selects other actors for their precise ability to fit such a scenario. In the marvelous line of Jean Kerr's play, *Mary, Mary*, "Some people are so good at making the best out of a bad situation that they go around creating bad situations that they can make the best out of."

‡ *Ibid.*, p. 159.

The loser will then seek friends who are most likely to guarantee yet greater and more spectacular losses. Marriage is a marvelous opportunity for losing. Indeed, the loser's unconscious deliberately selects a marriage partner who will guarantee him (or her) a long life of martyrdom. Indeed, if through some miracle, the marriage partner withdraws from the martyr role, then a new form of self-punishment is required. Thus it is not infrequent for the poor saintly woman who must put up with an alcoholic brute of a husband to herself become an alcoholic if the husband successfully resolves his problem. If she is no longer able to suffer because of his alcoholism, then she will degrade herself and suffer because of her own.

There is a strong urge in many people to lose in the friendship game. The levels of guilt, anxiety, aggression, resentment, and self-loathing in their personality are so high that systematic self-defeat seems to be the only possible strategy. Like Thomas E. Dewey in the famous 1948 election, they are under extreme pressure to snatch defeat from the jaws of victory. When someone comes close to them, seems on the verge of breaking through the defense mechanisms and destroying the pattern of habitual defeat, the loser reacts with violent hostility, and no effort must be spared in the attempt to convert the other into a substitute for the hated parent. It requires an extraordinarily strong and self-possessed person to resist such an onslaught from a determined loser.

There are two major strategies that losers favor. The first, and more masculine strategy, is vicious and vindictive punishment of the other. The more feminine approach is a form of clinging and demanding dependency that controls the other not so much by overpowering him as by bleeding the life out of him. In either case, the loser is about as safe for most of us as a rattlesnake. He has had long practice at destroying relationships and destroying them in such a fashion as to make the other look bad. We get involved with them at considerable peril.

The judgment may sound harsh. For most of us, the best thing we can do is avoid the loser. We are no match for him unless we have self-possession far above the normal, and we must be especially wary of him because his initial approach to relationships frequently makes him seem very seductive. He seems so pathetically in need of our help and so eager to respond to that help when it is first offered. But his initial reaction to us is simply part of his well-directed scenario. No matter how much he may appeal to our altruism, we ought to give him a wide berth.

Most of us are not losers, at least not inveterate and incurable losers, and yet there is a streak of the loser in our personality. We ought to ponder the loser in our reflections on friendship not so much to protect ourselves against losers but, rather, to recognize the loser in ourself. To what extent, we should wonder, have the failures in our friendships with others been rooted in a need for self-defeat and self-punishment? Do we make trouble in our friendships precisely because we are afraid of the risk-taking and the self-revelation in the friendship? Do we inflict punishment on our friend because we think we are not good enough for the friendship? Do we frustrate him and keep him at bay as a means of exercising power over him? Have we turned him into a surrogate parent on whom we can take out our pent-up aggressions? How much time and energy are we investing in allotting blame for the conflicts and tensions that arise in our friendship? How much time do we spend talking to others about his faults, trying to win confirmation and support from them for our battle against him?

The celibate in me is constantly astonished about the things that husbands and wives say about each other, frequently behind the back of the spouse, and sometimes in his presence. The complaints and criticisms may be made as though in jest, but they are far too serious and far too devastating to be jokes. The spouse wants his partner to look bad, to be humiliated and, if he wants to humiliate his partner, then he wants to punish himself. There is no better way to guarantee punishment than to humiliate a friend, and no better way to assure certain defeat in a relationship than to ridicule the partner in that relationship. Yet many husbands and wives seem to have perfected the art of mutual ridicule. Incredibly enough, they do not seem to understand what this ridicule reveals about themselves and their marriage. Perhaps the reason is that everybody else seems to engage in it, too. The suburban cocktail parties in which married couples vie with each other to see which couple can engage in the most impressive mutual flagellation were legend long before John Updike's *Couples*. The impressive thing about Updike's novel is that he managed to people it entirely with losers and still not let it deteriorate into slapstick farce.

The loser is a *homo Americanus*. Other societies have known him, of course, but our competitive, success-oriented, middle-class society has made the loser so frequent as to be almost typical. Karen Horney was correct when she observed several decades ago that the neurotic personality of our times was created by an absence of warmth and affection and love. In my own experience, those young people whose parents spent their formative years during the Great Depression are the ones most likely to be losers, most likely to be caught in the grip of a fierce demand for success and total absence of faith in their capacity for success. It is necessary not merely that they be successful in their careers, though that surely is expected, but they must be successful in everything they do. Their marriage relationship has to be a success both in bed and out, and all their friendships have to be successes, too. The very importance of success incapacitates and paralyzes them. Too much is riding on success, and therefore they would much prefer to lose without committing themselves to the pursuit of success. Even in marriage it is far better to hold oneself back and have available a ready excuse for failure than to commit oneself completely and fail without any excuse available. The loser is beaten not only before he walks onto the field, but even before he enters the park.

The reader may suspect that I've encountered a number of losers in my life in addition to watching the pathetic antics of the Chicago Cubs and the Chicago Bears and the Chicago Black Hawks on the television screen. The suspicion is a valid one. Sometimes, as a matter of fact, I am convinced that I have dealt with a whole generation of losers. Most of the young people with whom I have worked in my life are not risk-takers. They differ only in the degree to which they seem committed to imposing defeat after defeat upon themselves. They have been astonishingly successful in choosing marriage partners who will guarantee them long lives of frustration—and, of course, be frustrated in return.

It is by no means impossible for a loser to become a winner, sometimes even a big winner, and hence a good friend. I am not sure exactly what the difference is between losers who become winners and losers who remain losers, but the former seem usually to have greater vitality, more of a zest for life, perhaps even more animal energy. The incurable losers seem to have been born weary, apathetic, and stodgy. Their voice is a whine, their greatest show of emotion a yawn, their most frequent form of expression an excuse, but beneath an external style that is almost totally without affect, they are bitter, injured, envious, angry, vindictive men and women, incapable of authentic friendship or authentic creativity and productivity unless there is either a miracle or extensive psychotherapy.

76

LOSING IN THE FRIENDSHIP GAME

A society that will persist in producing a large number of such losers among its most talented young people is not a society in which friendship can be expected to flourish—not, at least, without very great difficulty.

77

7

FRIENDSHIP AS RHYTHM AND PLAY

The world outside the prison bars of shame and distortion turns out to be a playground, a vast splendid playground in the middle of which is a band shell and a dance floor; on the band shell a jazz combo is engaging in intricate musical patterns, and on the dance floor strong, vigorous, and handsome couples are working out complex patterns of movement. The combo in our playground is working hard because the musicians must keep in mind not only the melody that they are developing but also the melodic processes that their colleagues are working on. They must know their colleagues' talent and inclinations well enough to be able to judge from the past and the present of the melody where it is going to go in the future. Their ears must be keen; their emotions sensitive; their imagination free; and their creativity ingenious, for the harmony of the combo only survives as long as each of the players is able to be fully himself and at the same time fully in rapport with the others.

Similarly, on the dance floor the dancer must be conscious of the movements of his own body and at the same time be carefully observing the signals coming from the body of the other. Eyes, facial expressions, voice, touch, breathing, muscle movement—all are signs not merely of where the other dancer is now but of where he is going. The partner is so attuned to the movements of his colleague that their mutual movements become almost the movements of one person. The adjustment to the other's changing pattern is integrated effortlessly into one's own movements. Just as the jazz combo produces one harmony, so the two dancers produce one set of movements, not indeed by submerging themselves but, on the contrary, by being themselves for and with each other.

Friendship then is rhythm, an alternation of mood, sentiment, emotion, body, and soul, a constant passing of melody and harmony, of movement and countermovement from one partner to the other, a flow of signal and countersignal that enables each partner to be more fully himself and to facilitate the enrichment of the other. It is not a relationship in which there are any fixed rules or maxims. The only stability is the commitment to the motion itself, but within that commitment the roles, the rhythms, and the movements constantly ebb and flow.

But if we look at our jazz combo or our dancers in the middle of the park, we will discover that they are enjoying themselves. They are working hard, they are concentrating intensely, but they are also playing. What they are engaged in is far too serious to be taken seriously, far too important to be anything more than a game. The serious, well-organized, well-planned, rational world in which we work simply does not provide us with the freedom, the spontaneity, the relaxation that is necessary for friendship. Unless people are able to "let go" and be playful with one another, friendship doesn't stand a chance. As long as we remain serious, there is no way to escape inadequacy and shame, no way to break out of the foolishness of inauthentic encounter, no way to escape the distortion of the transference neurosis. If only we can frolic together when there is absolutely nothing serious that can be done, only then is friendship possible.

I was once part of a group of people who had embarked on the creation of a friendship community but who were trapped in a network of fear and hatred that was a re-creation of all their familial pasts. Many times this group of people would go to a place that was made to order for a playground, with water, sand, surf, boats, tennis courts, golf courses, and baseball fields all around, and yet they could not play together; the weekends at this splendid place were more dismal than wakes. Even though practically nothing happened on the weekends, and even though most of the members of the group would sleep ten hours each night, they would still go home on Sunday evening exhausted. If they had been able to play together, to take themselves and their fears less seriously, they might have become friends. But the terror of friendship was too great; they would not run the risk of terror by even attempting to play. If we get caught in the trap of play, there is no escape from it.

Similarly, one cannot help but be astonished (at least if one is a celibate watching from the outside) how little play there is between so many husbands and wives. Their relationship is dull, serious, and heavy. Humor, such as it is, tends to be bitter and based on ridicule of each other's faults. They are not good enough friends to play together and terrified of what play might lead to if they should give themselves over to it. Yet the marriage relationship is one which, by its very nature, is destined for play. The bodies of a man and a woman are meant to be played with by a member of the opposite sex. The constant incongruity of such an intimate relationship is almost necessarily hilarious; when children are added the hilarity becomes virtually irresistible—save for the fact that so many people have become so practiced in resisting anything as joyous as play or laughter. When one stops to think how systematic and effective the resistance is to play and hilarity in marriage, one realizes how deep our fears of intimacy really are and how powerful and resourceful are the defense mechanisms that we build up against friendship.

Rhythm requires playfulness, and play has a rhythm all its own. The rhythm of play is not learned easily, even though it looks easy when we see it in practice. A professional football team, a ballet troupe, a husband and wife who have become practiced at challenging and stimulating one another make it all look so very easy, and yet tremendous effort and practice—and many mistakes and blunders—have gone into the acquiring of their effortless playfulness. If the football players or the ballet dancers or the married lovers had quit because they made fools of themselves through their early blunders, the smooth harmony that we see could never have come into being. Friends who give up trying to obtain the playful rhythm that is required for mutual growth are cowards. Having risked a little bit of themselves and being rewarded only with partial success, they are disappointed and disillusioned. Either they must have instant success or they wish to quit. They are not strong enough to pick themselves off the ground after a failure and go back into the huddle to call another play.

In the jazz combo the lead melody passes effortlessly from one instrument to another, and in the dance first one partner and then the other plays the leading role. Similarly, in friendship, we who are friends with one another alternate taking the lead in the relationship. At one moment we surrender, and at another moment we conquer. At one moment we seduce; at another moment we let ourselves be seduced. At one moment we support; at another moment we seek support. At one moment we are very fragile and vulnerable;

81

at another moment, very strong and firm. At one moment we conquer; at another moment we yield. At one moment we dominate; at another moment we are passive. At one moment we challenge, and at another moment we respond to challenge. The ecstasy of the relationship is perhaps to be found most completely in the very fact of the alternation of roles. Conquest is made sweeter by the thought that in a moment we will be conquered, and surrender is made more delightful by the fact that we know that in a moment the other will surrender to us.

All of which is merely a somewhat poetic way of saying that in a friendship the moods and the roles and the emphases should never be linked to one partner. Friendship cannot exist if one person does all the living and the other all the getting. We may have a parent-child relationship or a dependency relationship or a client-professional relationship, but we do not have a friendship if one partner is pre-eminently dominant and the other pre-eminently passive. That many relationships that pass as friendships or even as marriages are in fact dominant-passive, parent-child, give-or-get relationships need hardly be emphasized. There may even be a certain stability in these relationships because the neurotic needs of both partners are being met in what seems to be a relatively satisfactory way. However, whatever else these relationships may be, they are not friendships, because friendship can only exist between colleagues who are equal partners. The jazz combo is not a paternalistic symphony orchestra, nor are the pair of elegant dancers in fact a dancing school where one partner is teaching and the other partner is learning. Friendship is possible only between or among equals.

Yet there is a strong tendency to build into a friendship a division of labor that attributes to one partner a majority of the dominant roles and to the other, a majority of the passive roles. It makes things so much easier if one person does most of the giving and the other most of the getting; if one does most of the seducing and the other most of the being seduced. This tendency toward a division of labor is especially obvious in marriage where, in Western society, the man is expected to be the aggressor and the woman the one who surrenders, despite the fact that the sexual pleasure for the man is far more gratifying if there are strong elements of surrender in his aggression and for the woman, far more ecstatic if she is permitted to dominate her husband as well as to surrender to him.

There may be much greater genital payoff in a marriage relationship where the rhythm between yielding and conquering is not tied to a division of labor, but the risks involved in such a free-flowing relationship are very considerable. Hence, it seems much safer to ignore the desirability of androgyny in the marriage relationship. For only when a man is fully assured of his successful masculinity is he able to let the feminine dimension of his personality evolve. Only when the man knows that he can be strong and firm and vigorous is he free to be gentle, tender, sensitive, and passive. And it is only when a woman knows that she is capable of warmth, affection, tenderness, sensitivity, and reassurance can she commit herself also to be strong, aggressive, and bold. It is bad enough trying to be a man or a woman without adding also trying to be a human being.

But of course the full, mature human being is a combination of masculine and feminine elements. Strong, vigorous, resourceful and, at the same time, gentle, sensitive, maternal. In a healthy marriage the man learns from his wife the art of tenderness and the wife the art of boldness from her husband. He will become tender and soft because she not only demands it of him, not only refuses to permit him not to display these characteristics, but also teaches him how. Similarly, she will learn to be forceful, aggressive, and dominant because her husband gives her no other choice and is prepared to teach her what these characteristics mean. But each can play the role of teacher to the other only if an atmosphere of confidence and playfulness pervades the relationship. A man can find the courage to experiment with the "soft" elements in his personality when the situation in which he finds himself has a gamelike quality. Similarly, a woman is prepared to develop "hard" elements in her personality especially when she can do so with the reassurance that she is doing it because it enhances the fun of the game.

The androgynous personality does not run from self-revelation but rather exults in it. Nor is it terrorized by the prospects of delight but rather, quite frankly, wants all the delight it can possibly get. The need for androgyny in healthy sexual intercourse is so obvious that it hardly needs to be pointed out. Unless the rhythm of yielding and conquering in the marriage bed is a symbol of a very much more pervasive yielding and conquering in the whole marriage relationship, it not only does not mean much in the marriage bed but is not likely to survive very long. Furthermore, in friendships that are not marriage, the rhythm between the two partners is as important as it is in marriage and, in its own way, both requires and facilitates androgyny almost as much as marriage does.

So friendship, then, must be a comedy. If the laughter, the adventure, the excitement, the emotional release of the comic is taken out of friendship, then the risk of tragedy is very high. A friendship cannot have a happy ending unless it is transfused by play and comedy. It is a very serious business the two friends are engaged in, and that is why they have no choice but to be comedians.

A young wife who was going through a fairly difficult emotional problem paid a high compliment to her husband's reaction to the problem, "He takes me very seriously but he refuses to be troubled by my tears." The person of his wife, then, was sacred, to be treated with reverence and respect, but her tears were laughable. The young man was a very skillful lover who could laugh at her fears without laughing at the woman. Precisely because he could do this, he enhanced her self-esteem and made the fears look like the absurdities that they were. So it must be with all friends. We must be able to combine laughter and reverence. Our friend must be a constant source of amusement to us without our ever laughing at him. He must always be delightful without ever seeming foolish, and always a comedian but never a clown. The line, of course, is a thin one and we are bound to wander across it or permit ourselves to become a clown instead of a comedian but, like all other dimensions in friendship, what is important is not instantaneous perfection but the unimpaired willingness to start all over again.

Writers such as Sam Keen, Robert Neale, and Harvey Cox have recently emphasized that man is most truly man not when he is involved in the drab, mundane, serious, technocratic world in which he must work but rather when he has given himself over to wonder, play, and laughter. One might add to the observations of these authors that man can only be a friend when he is capable of admiration for delight, comedy, and laughter.

It is one of the sublime paradoxes of the human personality that comedy is a necessary prelude to ecstasy.

8

FRIENDSHIP THROUGH SILENCE

The contemplative life is in deep trouble in the modern world. Vocations to contemplative monasteries seem to have vanished. Many of those inside such monasteries are arguing that the doors must be opened and the rest of the world brought into the monastery. Group discussion has replaced reflection, and one is assured by all sorts of enthusiastic young people that conversation is the only form of prayer they need. We are in heaven in the secular city. We work out our destiny not by contemplation, much less by mysticism, but rather by throwing ourselves vigorously and enthusiastically into the human relationships that constitute the secular city. In a mythological world, where man still believed in the sacred, reflection and contemplation might have been in order, but in the modern world what we need instead is more T-groups. Contemplation is finished.

Or is it? Zen seems to be quite popular. A considerable number of young people on college campuses are spending long hours each day in reflection and contemplation. At the

University of Chicago the disciples of the silent Indian mystic, Maherbbaba, have widespread influence (to the obvious delight of the school administration which, while puzzled by quiet students, nevertheless is not about to complain). Mysticism, which was supposed to be dead, seems suddenly to be very much alive. Men have discovered that they need time to be alone to be silent if their involvement in the secular city is to be anything more than just shallow activism. The insistence of the old spiritual writers on the need for contemplation seems astonishingly enough to be empirically validated. Contemplative life, buried only yesterday, seems now to be alive and well and not just in Argentina. And Professor Harvey Cox has made the pilgrimage from the secular city to a place that sounds remarkably like Camelot:

> Christian hope suggests that man is destined for a City. It is not just any city, however. If we take the Gospel as well as the symbols of the Book of Revelation into consideration, it is not only a City where justice is abolished and there is no more crying, it is a City in which a delightful wedding feast is in progress, where laughter rings out, the dance has just begun, and the best wine is still to be served.*

A group of young men and women whom I know who had been deeply involved in discussion and activity decided that they wanted an "old-fashioned" retreat in which there were periods marked out for solitude and silence. Solitude was a painful but very helpful experience for them because it forced them to face how shallow and superficial much of their activity was and how afraid they were to take a good, hard look at their commitments and convictions. Solitude and silence are the only antidotes man has for superficiality. He

* Harvey Cox, *Feast of Fools*. New York, 1969.

who is unable to be quiet will never be anything else but shallow.

Silence is necessary for friendship. Not the silence of two people who say nothing to each other because they have nothing to say, or who refuse to communicate with each other because they have built up such effective barriers of anger and hatred, but rather the solitude of friends who are confident enough of their relationship that they do not have to talk about it or even talk about anything. On the contrary, such friends feel that by being together in silence and reflection they communicate to each other more deeply than they would with a thousand analytic conversations. We flee from delight, playfulness, comedy, and trust. If we once stop to reflect on things, if we pause to consider what is really happening we may be so frightened that we will have to change our behavior, and if we do that heaven knows what disasters are likely to befall us. If we can be silent with our friend then we may be forced to communicate with him, and if we communicate with him maybe our relationship may become a friendship and even a communion.

Husband and wife surround themselves with noise, bustle, and activity in their marriage precisely because if there were any silence they would either fight with one another or face each other and discover what strangers they are to one another. And if a man and woman find out that they are strangers after years of marriage, either their marriage is a failure, which may be an acceptable tragedy, or it may still have a chance of success, which could be a quite unacceptable comedy.

So silence then is to be avoided at all costs. Reflective, sensitive, probing silence is incompatible with superficiality, but superficiality is one of the best guarantees we have that we need not face either the terrors or the delights of friendship. If we practice authentic silence, then the conspiracy of silence into which we have contracted looks like the coverup that it really is. We must keep talking, keep making noise, keep surrounding ourself with hubbub if only because under such circumstances the conspiracy of silence is never questioned. We need not talk about the disappointments in our sexual relationship. We need not talk about the small aggravations or the big ones. We need not demand that the other have faith in himself. Only in the awesomeness of silence do these issues ever come to the surface. The silence of hurt or anger, of course, may be very useful, because under such circumstances our self-pity takes control, and self-pity is the best protector of shame, inadequacy, timidity, and fear that man has ever devised. But reflection, authentic silence, makes us realize how absurd self-pity is and forces us to ask what has happened to our dreams and whether perhaps there is something in us that weakens our friendships, blights our gifts, distorts our invitation, and causes us to renege on our promise. Small wonder that most of us can take so little of silence, particularly when it is silence shared with a friend; if the silence goes on too long we may in sheer desperation turn to the friend with a plea for help only to discover that at almost the same time he is turning to us with the same plea.

And then where would the two of us be?

It is necessary for friends to be alone together whether the friendship be dyadic or involve a community of people. And to be alone means really to be alone, to be cut off temporarily at least from interruption, from activity, from phone calls, from the office, from baby sitters. It does not mean sight seeing, or watching television, or reading the Sunday newspaper, or even listening to the car radio. It means rather silence, and silence alone with one another. For many partners in human relationships such isolated silence is an extraordinarily traumatic experience. They discover at first that they have very little to say to each other and then, if the silence endures long enough, that they have far more to say than the time will permit or their strength will sustain. How could a friendship go on so long with so many things unsaid? Why does it take silence to realize how many things we have been foolishly silent about? Why is it only in silence that we can give voice to the profound, moving affection we have for one another? Why do we have to withdraw from life to be able to begin to live? Why do we have to step aside from the world to find out that it is a playground with a band shell and a dance floor? Why is it that only in silence we learn to speak? Why is it in the midst of reflection that we are able to become comedians? Why is it that when we are alone, truly alone with one another, we discover the depths of our love not only for each other but for the whole world that we have presumably left behind, however temporarily?

The answers to these questions are as clear as they are disturbing. Only in silence and solitude can we strip ourselves of escapes, and only when we are alone with our friends in quiet together with them can we see clearly the barriers that still exist. To see those barriers clearly, and also to see the splendid opportunity beyond the barriers, the splendid people who are still heavily shrouded in veils, only then can we begin to realize the price we have to pay for letting terror triumph over delight. Many of us flee from silence precisely because we do not want to see either the veils or those who wear them.

I remember a retreat that one group of friends attempted. There were very considerable barriers separating them. The conflicts and the strains threatening their embryonic friendships were growing more intense. The retreat could easily have been a turning point in their relationships, but almost from the first minute they arrived, the attempts to prevent silence and reflection began. One of the members, in particular, who had paralyzing fears of intimacy, discovered a terribly important activity that was going to occupy him on the final day of the retreat, and so this young man spent the entire weekend making important phone calls concerning this impressive activity. His phone calls and preparations for the activity not only kept him from the awful challenge of silence, but effectively ruined the retreat weekend for everyone else in the group. But no one stopped him, partly because the group's culture at that time was such that any behavior, no matter how neurotic or disruptive, had to be tolerated, and partly because most of the other members of the group were grateful to the young man for protecting them from the challenge of silence. The weekend was a turning point for the group, a prelude to its destruction.

Solitude then is as necessary for friendship as is play. In fact, the two activities overlap. Solitude is most easy after we have exhausted ourselves playing together, and play, in its turn, can only exist when some sort of solitude liberates us from the superficiality and pseudoseriousness of mundane life. There is little solitude in many incipient friendships for the same reason that there is so little play. If we get caught in solitude we will be in the same difficulty we would be in if we were caught in play, for both in play and in silence we are forced to be ourselves, to put aside, however temporarily and however incompletely, distortions and the inauthenticity with which we protect ourselves from our friends. Shallow, superficial, dull, drab, dreary lives are not much fun. In fact, they're almost not worth living, but at least they are safe. At least we will not be found out; at least our inadequacy will not be discovered; at least no one will make demands upon us.

9

FRIENDSHIP AND DEMANDS

Among the more pernicious heresies of our time is "doing your own thing." According to this clever cop-out, all that matters is that we do what we want to do, that we be sincere, and that we don't hurt anyone else. If we are thus "doing our own thing," then no one has any right to interfere with us, not the law, and certainly not our friends. What counts is not so much whether what we are doing is good or bad, whether it is helping us or hurting us, but that we "know what we are doing." Exactly what that means may be open to question, because in very few instances are human beings fully aware of what they are doing. But as long as one can cover behavior with the label "they know what they're doing," both "they" and "we" are excused from any serious concern.

A young priest I know was counseling a very disturbed young woman who had moved into an apartment with her lover to set up a joint housekeeping venture that was bound to be an emotional disaster for the two of them. The young priest was very proud that he would not be disturbed by a little bit of casual fornication and felt no need to point out to the young girl that whatever the issues of sexual morality that might be involved in her relationship, there was not much doubt that it was bound to do immense harm to her psyche and that of her friend. That, thought this priest-counselor, was none of his affair, and so he openly encouraged the relationship, explaining this to me by asserting "it's all right; the two of them know what they are doing."

They most assuredly did not know what they were doing, and the subsequent tragedy of their relationship was evidence enough of this, but the point of the story is that the young priest thought he was playing the role of friend by not warning the young woman of the trouble she was getting into. We must love our friends, no matter what foolish things they do, but to love them despite their folly is something less than to encourage them in the folly, or to give passive approval by our silence. Friendship, quite the contrary, demands that we challenge our friends to be who and what they really are without ever implying in the challenge a withdrawal of our affection for them. It is not an easy art to practice, mostly because the challenges that we receive in our life as we grow up usually are offered as conditions for love. A challenge that is not a condition for love, but the result of it, is both hard to give and hard to receive, but in any friendship worth the name, challenges and demands are inevitable elements in the relationship.

In the popular psychology of our time, it is argued that friends make no demands, and that a friend's response to his partner's behavior should be one of "total acceptance." When someone challenges a friend or confronts him (at least outside the T-group culture), those who look on remark in horrified shock, "Is that any way to treat a friend?" The only response to such a question is, "It is the only way to treat a friend."

93

Friendship, then, demands that we make demands. It demands that we require that the other reveal himself to us, that he honor his promise to us, that he does not pull back on the gift he has offered us, that he does not renege on his invitation. And just as we must make demands on our friends to honor their commitments to us, so we have no choice but to expect that our friends will demand that we honor our commitments to them.

The necessity of demands in friendship is particularly obvious if we look at the marriage friendship. The husband must challenge his wife to be a woman, he must demand that she respond to him as a woman responds to a man. If she is trapped in either physical or psychological frigidity, he must demand that she break out of it. His demands are of course gentle, tender, sensitive, and reassuring, but they are also insistent. If he does not make such demands, he is simply not a male. He has allowed his wife to use her frigidity as a weapon to emasculate him. Similarly, a wife must require of her husband that he not be so committed to his professional career that he be incapable of being a married lover. If the career becomes a demanding mistress to whom she may very well lose her husband, then the wife must seduce him back to her marriage bed. Her demands then with him must be discreet, subtle, and delicate, but absolutely imperious. If she does not make such demands on her husband, then she is no longer a woman.

I must remark in passing how astonished I am at how many women seem so easily to lose their husbands to the mistress of his professional career. It is a rare woman who is not fully aware of her husband's psychological and physical Achilles heel. She can, if she is of such a mind, very quickly and easily reduce him to a condition of panting, trembling jelly which she can gently hold in her hands, and yet she so often refuses to do so. If her husband wishes to choose the career over her, far from seducing him back, she will become aloof and haughty, demanding that if there is to be any tenderness between them he must take the initiative instead of she. One can only conclude that she wants to lose to the career. If she should win in the battle with her husband's career, she might have him on her hands and in her hands for the rest of their life together, and she's not so sure that that would be altogether a good thing.

We must therefore demand in all our friendships that the friend be who he really is. No matter how hard he tries to put aside our demands, no matter how cleverly he manipulates our neurotic weaknesses to turn our demands into replications of parental demands, we must then insist that we have complete respect for his freedom and no intention of withdrawing our affection, but also that we have no intention of settling for anything less than the excellence of which he is capable. We do not demand the excellence of productivity or of achieving, but rather excellence of being, and our demand for this is simple, categoric, and unnegotiable. It's not necessary that the friend achieve this excellence in being today or tomorrow, or even in its perfection, ever, but it is necessary that he begin, that he acknowledge that he is afraid of it and that he respond not with anger or fear but with gratitude and affection for our demand.

Therefore, just as married lovers in the heat of their passion cannot tolerate the garments that stand as a barrier, however flimsy, to their total availability to each other, so all friends must demand of one another that the rigid, opaque barriers set up by our fears, our anxieties, our dreads, and our defense mechanisms be stripped away. We know that the defense mechanisms do not collapse at once. We are well enough aware of our own to understand that. But we must also insist that the process begin. While we guarantee our friend that we will be patient, we also guarantee to him that

95

we expect honesty and that we persist in our absolute refusal to be put off by the tricks and the games that he will try to play with us.

One of the major difficulties in making such demands —or in responding to them, for that matter—is that there is always a gnawing fear that the demand may not be a valid one, that we may have misunderstood the friend, that he may not really be the person we think he is, and that what we are demanding of him may be in fact a neurotic trick of our own personality. Obviously, when we begin to think in these terms we have gotten ourselves into a very complicated situation. But then life is a very complicated situation, and we must be aware of the fact that what looks to us like authentic demands of true friendship may in fact be just one more form of neurotic self-defense. If this is a possibility that we cannot easily dismiss, it ought not to be a possibility that paralyzes us completely. We must be wary of our instincts, particularly when we know that some instincts are deeply connected with our own emotional problems, but, on the other hand, we have no choice in human life but to trust our instincts. If the relationship is basically a sound and healthy one, the powerful instincts we have about it that correspond to the real world in which we and the friend live, can usually be trusted.

I wrote the previous paragraph as one who must confess having been periodically paralyzed by such twisted doubts. So often I have asked myself, "Is this challenge that I make to a friend really a valid challenge? Is it really something that I not only can, but must ask of him? Is it really something that the best in his personality wishes I would ask?" I will admit that, on some occasions, such convoluted anxieties have forced me to be silent. But, as I review such situations in my mind, it seems fairly clear to me that at those times when I was feeling confidence in myself, when I had faith in my own convictions about who and what I was, my instincts about what to demand of others were valid. It was only when my own selfhood was under doubt, when I lost confidence in my own goodness and integrity that the style, if not the actuality of my demands was mistaken. I conclude, therefore, that with time and practice we learn how to read our own instincts and to know which are valid, which are dubious, and which are dangerously close to neurotic.

But even when we are as certain as we can be of the validity of our demands, it is still difficult to make them, both because the combination of patience and tenderness with insistence and firmness that such demands must display is not easy to come by, and because our friend is very likely to have a whole set of clever defenses to deflect our demands.

I must confess that I feel very little confidence in my own ability to combine tenderness and firmness. What often comes out is merely watered-down firmness that displays rather little gentleness. I am, in other words, very good at challenging and much less good at comforting, which, be it noted, is a very serious handicap for anyone presuming to be a Catholic priest. Curiously enough, or perhaps not so curiously considering the chemistry of sexuality, I am much better at challenging women than men, for with women I can be gentle and tender and supportive while at the same time being insistent and demanding, but I have no idea how to be gentle and tender with other men. However, I take some courage in the thought that few men in our society do know how to combine masculinity with tenderness.

There are two basic defense systems that our friend is likely to establish against our demands. In the first he will attempt to set up a different set of rules, and in the second he will react with hostility.

The attempt to legislate special rules is as subtle as it is insidious. The friend will plead weakness, fragility, vulnerability. He'd like so much to be what we want of him, but the demand we make on him is paralyzing. Because he is so weak, so vulnerable, so easily hurt, he must plead exemption from the rules of friendship. We can make demands on him only occasionally, only very indirectly, and only with no insistence. The harried, harassed, compulsive housewife, for example, must be excused from our demands because she is a harried, harassed, incompetent housewife. Poor housewife. She is so befuddled, so bedraggled, and so worthless that only the most cruel tyrant could harden his heart to demand anything of her. She can keep her husband at bay and everyone else, too. Her husband feels sorry for her, does everything he can to ease her burdens (most of which she has created herself), and studiously refrains from demanding anything from her, even love-making. She has used her weakness, her fragility, her vulnerability as means of imposing powerful control on him and on everyone else who gets close to her.

Her first cousin is the woman with an outraged sense of justice and a powerful capacity for anger. Nobody dares to challenge her or make demands on her because she will lash back, not merely in anger, but in anger that condemns the challenger to judgment of all who are in earshot. Since she is such a powerful maternal figure and is able to stir up childhood guilt feelings in most of her associates, her condemnations are feared by one and all; no one dares to dispute them, not even to himself. She is a powerful woman and controls those around her, and lives in a very lonely, isolated, unpleasant world.

The fierce-tempered matron and the poor befuddled housewife have both succeeded in establishing special rules for themselves. So frequently too do their husbands who are important professional men on whom many people depend for their safety and welfare. We don't dare challenge the professional man (especially if he is a doctor), because to demand anything of him is interpreted that he abandon the sacred responsibility he has to his clients or his colleagues. He would rather like to be a human being someday, but just now he really couldn't do so without failing in his professional responsibilities. So he, too, sets up rules of his own.

Then there is the self-confessed neurotic—the person who has learned how to play the therapy game and to use the alleged advice of his therapist (frequently edited into saying exactly the opposite of what the therapist said) to control others and to prevent them from making demands on him (or her). "I would really like to respond to your demand," says the player of the neurotic game, "but I'm afraid I can't because you see I'm a neurotic and I have this complex about you and my therapist says now I can't possibly do anything else but go along with the complex."

When one encounters such excuses, one is reminded of the scriptural story about those who were invited to the wedding feast. They would really liked to have gone, but they had such splendid excuses and, hence, they asked that the ordinary rules of human etiquette and friendship be waived and that they be held excused from attending the wedding feast. When they got tossed into the darkness outside they received what they richly deserved.

The alternative defense against our demands is to attack us, make demands on us that seem merely to reciprocate the demands that we have made on the friend. It seems so fair and so just that if he permits us to demand something of him we would permit him to make similar demands on us and, indeed, in many circumstances it would be eminently fair and just. But the demands on us that are made as defenses against us are vague, unspecific, punitive, and hateful. The nastier they are the better they are to serve the unconscious purpose for which they exist. So we want to play a game of making demands, do we? Very well, two can play at the same game. The game will be made so rough and so vicious that we will very quickly tire of it and give it up if not completely withdraw from the relationship.

The closer we get to breaking through the last barriers of terror which our friend has wrapped around himself the more punitive and vindictive his demands on us may be. He may even be prepared to admit when we catch him off guard that he is making punitive demands on us precisely to keep us at bay. As a last desperate defense against openness and trust, he uses a caricature of the demands of friendship to keep friendship from becoming a reality. Either we display rigid flexibility and open firmness or we permit the other to push us away and turn what might have been a friendship into bitter enmity.

There are some sets of circumstances where we are simply not strong enough to break through and perhaps no one else is either. But there are other times, I fear, when we could break through if we were only a bit more patient, if we could only combine more firmness and more tenderness with a refusal to take seriously the hatred and the anger we hear from our potential friend. I am well aware that some relationships in which I am no longer involved never had a chance in the beginning, but I am also afraid that there are some which I turned away from at the last moment when, if I could have kept my cool for a few more hours or a few more days or a few more weeks, I would have had a friend for life. It is now far too late.

In the previous paragraphs I have described the demand-making relationship in terms of our making our demand on the other, but reality usually involves two-way demands, with both sides making realistic and neurotic demands simultaneously and both partners trying to filter out the reality from the unreality. It is to be feared that we do not even have the conceptual apparatus to describe this most awkward and difficult part of the dance of friendship.

The very core of friendship, then, is the ability to make demands. He who knows how to make demands of a friend will have many friends and will be deeply loved; he who does not have enough self-confidence, enough trust in his instincts, enough willingness to risk all, to insistently demand response from his friends will, it is much to be feared, have no friends at all. It is hard to say whether yielding to a friend's demands or making demands on him contain more terrors, but at least by yielding to the demands we do not risk the end of friendship; we merely risk the exposure of our worthlessness. By making a demand on the other we do risk the end of friendship, and sometimes we gamble all on the throw of the dice and lose.

10

THE LIMITATIONS OF FRIENDSHIP

By now it should be clear that I am convinced that only paradox enables us to describe friendship adequately. It is terrifying and delightful, free and demanding, deadly serious and a great comedy. The most difficult thing in life, it is the gift of the total self and yet requires that we impose strict limitations. We give ourself to each other in friendship without condition or reservation but, at the same time, we draw a line around ourself which we refuse to let anyone cross, even the friend; one might say, especially the friend.

In the watered-down version of the Christian spiritual tradition in which I was trained in the seminary years, there was still much wisdom but, with the wisdom, there was also a good deal of foolishness. Some of the worst of the foolishness was that which made a virtue out of self-contempt. We were taught, sometimes successfully and sometimes not, to despise ourselves, to quote Scripture out of context and proudly announce, "I'm a worm and no man." We came to believe that virtue consisted in making ourselves completely and totally available to others. We were urged to turn the other cheek, forgetting that the man who gave us that advice could be quite fiery in his condemnations and quite fierce in defense of himself. The meek who we believed would inherit the earth came out sounding like doormats. It made for wonderful social control and produced parrots whom pastoral tyrants could dominate and intimidate. It, alas, did not produce adult human beings who could make decisions, take responsibility, and sustain themselves in times of crisis and confusion with strong internalized commitments and convictions. It also did not train us very well for friendship, because no one ever told us in the seminary that a doormat cannot be a friend.

In the previous chapter I suggested that we must make ourselves available to the demands of our friends, and in this chapter I am saying that some demands must be resisted, but the paradox is not as outrageous as it may seem. When we impose limitations on our friends we are, in effect, simply making the most important demand that we can make, and that is the demand that the friend respect the integrity of our selfhood. We will gladly yield ourselves to him in complete surrender so long as we yield ourself as human beings, with dignity and integrity; but if he demands that we give up our integrity, our privacy, our freedom, and belong so totally to him that we become not more than human but less than human, we must bluntly refuse.

In theory it is easy to distinguish between the two kinds of demands—the demand of friendship that liberates us and makes us more fully ourself and the demand for dependency that imprisons us and makes us less fully ourself. Unfortunately, in practice it is often hard to distinguish between the two, especially since the two kinds of demands can become confused with one another. We are therefore forced to become skilled in separating the signals that our friend is send-

ing us from the static that interferes with the signals. It is
the signals from his authentic self to our authentic self that
liberate us; it is the static of neurotic, regressive demands
that may imprison both of us. We must be able to habitually
ask ourself at the preconscious level which kind of demands
come from the best of him to the best of us; from the most
authentic in him to the most authentic in us; and which come
from his defense system, designed to appeal to our own
neuroses. If the sort of surrender that he requires is authentic,
then yield we must, however painful it may seem. If, on the
other hand, the two of us would become less ourselves should
we surrender to his demands, then reality is being violated,
and both of us will suffer.

Reality must then be the ultimate norm. Who are we
in reality and who is he? What is the reality of our relationship? These questions are easy to ask, but in the tumult and
passion and confusion of an emerging friendship they are
frequently not so easy to answer. We have not yet developed
the signals and the codes that will make clear communica-
tion between our authentic selves possible. The only tools we
have available are gentleness, tenderness, and patience and,
while these are indispensable tools, they are no substitute for
experience. Nothing is ever lost in friendship by a gentle response, and nothing is ever gained by an angry response. But
it is, unfortunately, precisely at the time when we are most
likely to be confused, when we find it most difficult to separate the authentic from the inauthentic, the real from the unreal in our relationships, that we are likely to be afraid of
tenderness and gentleness and to fall back on the stern defense
of anger and punishment.

In my own life, resisting the neurotic demands of others,
particularly when those others depend on me in one way or
another, is extremely difficult. Although I think I am a little
better now than I used to be at resisting such demands, I still

am not very good at it. Either I furiously and angrily reject the demand or accept the unreality the demander wishes to impose on me and store away my anger for eruption on another day, the day when the occasion for the anger may be very mild indeed.

To be able to reject neurotic demands without rejecting the friend who makes the demand requires a strong sense of one's own selfhood, the kind of sense of selfhood of the young man I mentioned in an earlier chapter who could take his wife very seriously but her fears and anxieties not seriously at all. One must also have a strong sense of the basic reality of the relationship of whom the two people are, what common purpose binds them together, what roles and values they share. But even with such an awareness of one's own selfhood, and of the adventure on which the self and the friend have embarked, it is still difficult to say "No" to the other's demands when they are patently neurotic and especially when the other still depends upon us for support and help.

I suppose it is a built-in trap for the clergyman, whose mission it is to be available for others when they need someone to lean on. From being the father who supports it is so very easy to become the father-figure who is responsible. The borderline between paternal support and paternalistic domination is thin. And when one begins to assume that one is responsible for the ultimate fate of someone else, then that border has been crossed. I must acknowledge that I have crossed it many more times than once in my own life—and sometimes have been intolerably slow in scurrying back.

I have a strong tendency to yield to neurotic demands, particularly when I am tempted to feel responsible for the other. It is so much easier, it takes so much less time, it avoids confusion and difficulty and, at least in the short run, there is less strain. I am also very well aware that when I attempt to respond to a neurotic demand by asserting my own reality,

I will very quickly make the pilgrimage from self-assertion to the defense mechanism of a pyrotechnic temper. To assert my integrity and validity in the face of the other's neurotic demands involves the risk of losing control of a very considerable amount of Celtic fury that I seem to have inherited from my ancestors. Particularly if I am tired or distracted or harassed or deeply involved in my work, it is very difficult to assert my integrity to resist a demand and still control my temper.

I would rather not have to put in the effort, at least not today. I would rather not have to slow down everything else to make quite explicit to myself that this neurotic and unreal demand that is being made on me is a sign of fear and anxiety, a plea for reassurance and love. It is particularly difficult when I find that the other is trying to turn me from the father that my ministerial role makes me to a father-figure that he would dearly like to have both to depend on and to hate. I am not a father-figure, I am not the parent with whom he still has unresolved problems, I do not want to take away his freedom, I do not want to dominate him but I wish to hell he'd leave me alone with his silly neurotic fixations. I have other and better things to do than to try to fend off his sly innuendos about my wanting to dominate his life and control his destiny. I don't give a damn about his life and destiny; I want him to be a free, adult human being, and the sooner he becomes that the happier I will be. So, sonny, go away and stop bothering me. And if it happens to be a woman instead of a man, the dismissal may be a little bit slower in coming and a little more gentle when it does come, but the lady is by no means immune from the Celtic temper tantrum either.

Since, as I promised in the Introduction, this is not my memoirs, I will not engage in any detailed analysis of the origins of this inclination to fury when I find myself caught in somebody else's neurotic demands. Suffice it to say that I am very well aware that there is nothing more calculated to reinforce his neurosis than my fury and that his unconscious is hoping against hope that I will respond with anger. Those who are psychoanalytically sophisticated can make their own judgments about what childhood experiences incline me to this sort of reaction, and those who are not should at least be assured that I have some awareness of what is going on.

The point of this excursion into my own hangups is to illustrate how passivity and inertia incline us to be doormats, to yield our own dignity and integrity to neurotic demands of others for the sake of temporary peace and serenity. We will punish the other by sulking (at which, God help me, I am an expert) and eventually become livid with rage. Whatever short-run benefits there are to being a doormat, the long-run costs make it a very unproductive strategy, but that doesn't mean that we don't keep on following the strategy.

As in so many other elements in friendship, the line that we must draw is a very delicate one. On one side of the line there is a defensiveness and insecurity and, on the other, the calm, cool assertion of our reality, the reality of the other person, and the reality of our relationship with one another. The line is also drawn between confidence in our own integrity, coupled with an awareness of our own unconscious needs on the one hand and harshness, arrogance, and insensitivity on the other. We may as well face the sorry fact that we are likely to stray over the line more than once in any friendship. In fact, we are likely to cross the line many times. The answer, as in any other problem in friendship, is the willingness to start over again and the realization that if the other is forced to be patient with our blunders so we, too, are forced to be patient with his.

The sensitivity enthusiasts are fond of the phrase, "total availability." Though it is not altogether clear what they mean by the phrase, many of the sensitivity cultists act as though total availability is to be taken with strict literalness, particularly when it is *someone else's* total availability that is at issue. While there are some interpretations of the phrase that are perfectly acceptable, I am inclined to think that as it stands it could easily be misleading. The distinction between the doormat and the totally available person is not altogether clear. I would prefer then to speak of *real* availability. By this I mean availability rooted in respect for our own dignity and integrity with an awareness of what is most authentic in our friend and what is most appropriate in the relationship between the two of us. Total availability is simple enough to apply in practice; real availability involves difficult and very tentative decisions, decisions which, after they have been made, may frequently turn out to have been quite wrong. But the mature person knows that he must make choices and must assume responsibility for the choices even though the information available for decision-making is hardly adequate. "Total availability," like all other simplistic solutions, eliminates the need for analysis, interpretation, and choice. It provides the magic answer to fit all situations. It assumes that the world is black or white, but, alas, the world is gray. We must make choices, and some of them will inevitably be wrong. On occasion, such wrong choices may severely damage, if not terminate, relationships that are moving toward friendship. There isn't much we can do about it, save to lament the ambiguity and the uncertainty of the human condition. We must do our best to be true to ourselves and what seem to be our most authentic insights and instincts. When we make mistakes, the best we can do is try to learn from them though frequently the fact that we have learned much from the mistake is small consolation.

And so we must decide, frequently on the spur of the

moment and on the basis of instinct alone, which demands are to be yielded to with terror and delight and which ones are to be vigorously resisted as an infringement of our integrity and dignity. We make mistakes. We hope that with the passage of time, the mistakes are less frequent.

11

FRIENDSHIP AND SELFHOOD

I am afraid that most of the previous chapters of this book have made friendship sound like a twisted and agonized process. I would not want to deny that the road to friendship is a difficult and obscure one. If friendship were easy, there would be a lot more of it in the world, but there is more to friendship than the difficulty of sustaining the rhythm of the dance with our partner. Perhaps because a social analyst looks for difficulties and perhaps because of the experiences at the present time in my life, I have emphasized the terror more than the delight, the anguish more than the ecstasy, but make no mistake about it, friendship is delightful. It is ecstatic. The only reason we are willing to pay the price for friendship is because the payoff is so great. Friendship is a distracting, enervating, wearying process. It threatens our integrity, it leaves our dignity open to violation, it makes life complex, confused, and uncertain, but there is no other way to be a human being.

W. H. Auden has said very beautifully that the ego

is but a dream until our neighbors need my name to find it. In the dance of friendship we discover not only the friend but also the self. Friendship is the only way that we can come to see the riches of our own possibilities, when the admiration for those possibilities is so powerfully reflected in the face of our friend that we can no more escape it than we can the glare of the rising sun. Friendship forces us to be ourself because it forces us to live up to our promise to the friend. Friendship, indeed, seduces us into being ourself. If, somehow or other, we do lose ourself instead of gaining ourself in friendship, it is not because our defenses were too weak to keep the other out but because they were strong enough to keep us in.

There is an electricity about a friendship relationship. We are both more relaxed and more sensitive, more confident and more vulnerable, more creative and more reflective, more energetic and more casual, more excited and more serene. It is as though when we come in contact with our friend we enter into a different environment where the air we breathe is more pure, the sounds we hear are sharper, the colors we see more dramatic, and the ideas we think quicker and more inciteful. The physical environment, of course, is not different at all, but the psychosocial environment is completely different, because now we are in a situation not only where we are free to be ourselves but where we have no choice.

The process may not be as quick or as spectacular as that which can be produced by narcotics or alcohol but it is, in the long run, both more satisfying and more permanent. If human beings need drugs to turn them on it is probably because they do not have any friends. It is the function of our friends to turn us on, and if our acquaintances do not do so then they probably are not our friends.

If we need to create trust by chemicals, if we can only overcome the terror of our aloneness by playing games with our physiology, then the friendship environment in our life must be sadly deficient. I know of a group of Catholics who have a "marijuana mass." The priest and community smoke pot after the homily in order that they might be turned on for the rest of the mass (given the quality of homilies heard in the Roman Catholic Church today the marijuana ought to be used, if it is going to be used at all, before the homily instead of after). These people are not the first ones to use artificial stimulants to enhance their liturgical worship but, as I understand the Christian liturgical tradition, the Communion banquet is supposed to be an agape, a love feast in which people are turned on precisely by their commitment to one another in charity. In the Epistle to the Corinthians, St. Paul had some rather harsh judgments to make about those who needed artificial stimulus in order to be able to display their love for one another. Friendship was expected in the Christian community, and hence no artificial stimulant was required for ecstasy.

The disadvantages of friendship as a stimulant are many. It doesn't produce instant ecstasy. It requires effort and practice and, worst of all, we cannot do it by ourselves. To light up a reefer, to swallow an LSD cube, to inject heroin into our bloodstreams, or to consume a pitcher of martinis is essentially an individual act, even though we may engage in such an act in the presence of others. We do not need anyone else's cooperation to get "high." We can escape from the human pack (and perhaps climb back to our tree in the jungle) with the drug. Artificial ecstasy enables us to turn away from our fellow human beings. Friendship, on the other hand, does not exist at all unless it exists in communion with other human beings. In friendship, the other turns us on and we are, in an existential and not psychological sense, dependent on him. It is the haughty, independent, arrogant, secular man who needs chemical ecstasy. In fact, he not only has no friends, he wants none, and as for the next morning's hangover, it is at least better than being stuck permanently with another human being who is likely to make insistent and embarrassing demands on him.

Friendship is a bursting out, a breaking of chains, a tossing aside of shackles, a liberation from bonds. We may not even realize until we have broken out of them that we were caught in shackles. The prison bars may exercise their restraints on us precisely because they remain invisible, but when our friend invites and then seduces us to break out of the bars, the experience of smashing through them, however painful, is also exhilarating.

Friendship is a game, a game that demands stamina and vigorous exercise. We pant with exhaustion, but it is a good feeling of exhaustion, that feeling that comes after an exercise that has challenged us, stimulated us, brought forth spectacular energies from us, reassured us of our vigor and strength and potency, and ended in victory. And the nice thing about the friendship game is that both sides win. The exhaustion of friendship, then, may make us tired, but it does not make us weary. There may be pain in our muscles, but there is also a sense of power in them. Our breath may come in heavy spurts, but our lungs are filled with fresh air. We enjoy the respite of the time out, but we want to get back into the huddle and resume the game again.

Friendship, as I said at the beginning of the book, is love and, like all other love, requires faith and hope; indeed, friendship produces ecstasy in us precisely because its love challenges our faith and our hope to the ultimate in their resources.

The faith that is required for friendship is the belief that it is safe to love and to accept love. My own religious beliefs lead me to speculate that the faith is necessarily rooted in some commitment to the ultimate graciousness of Being. One can only run the risk of believing that love is possible when one believes, however implicitly, that Creation is not absurd but is rather a gift to be accepted. Since such a theological question is beyond the scope of the present book, it is sufficient to say that friendship requires a tentative commitment to the notion that human intimacy is possible and rewarding and that we are human enough to be capable of intimacy.

Such a commitment involves a gigantic leap beyond the empirical data, beyond the positive evidence, beyond the barriers of the timid self. There is ample evidence that friendship does not work and fairly convincing evidence that no one could possibly like us. We are tempted to do on the personal level what the logical positivist philosophers do on the metaphysical level. It is much easier to analyze language instead of risking ourselves in encounter with the mysterious other. We must make a mighty leap of faith to say that friendship is possible for us and even may be rewarding—indeed, ecstatically rewarding. I think that such a leap is probably more difficult than the leap of faith that brings us to that Being that is the ground of all other beings.

My colleague, Van Cleve Morris, in his book, *Existentialism in Education,* notes that the existentialist believes that he must live in such a way that if nothingness is the result of human life it would be an unjust sentence. This is a heroic leap of faith that contains within itself a commitment to the graciousness of Being, however implicit, that many explicit theists are not capable of making. I suspect that Dean Morris might not want to see quite as many implicit commitments in the existentialist leap as I would, but I think that we would both agree that on the level of human interaction, the only appropriate approach to friendship is the existentialist one. We must act in the friendship relationship in such a way that if rejection is the response to us then it would be an unjust response. We must make a powerful enough commitment of faith to our own goodness, to the possibility of friendship, and to the goodness of the other that the failure of friendship cannot be attributed to the timidity of our faith.

Such faith both generates and requires hope. Gabriel Marcel, the French Christian existentialist, says that hope is the radical refusal to put limits to the possible. It is precisely this kind of existentialist hope that is involved in both the cause and effect of friendship. We are aware, of course, that we are limited creatures and that somewhere there are limits to the things that are possible for us. But we will not permit premature closure of our possibilities. We will not draw the lines until we have fully tested our competencies. Interpersonal hope requires that we refuse to put limits on the possibility of trust and self-revelation in our relationship with our friends. At no point will we say that trust has gone so far and can go no farther; at no time will we say that both of us have developed to the fullest our capacity for love, and need not push ahead any farther. At no point will we say that the light is so ecstatic that we cannot bear any more of it, nor at any time will we say that the terror of intimacy is now so overpowering that we will go no farther.

We would like very much to believe that is the strong human being who refuses to lose control of himself, who always holds some of himself back. But the man who holds himself back from the authentic encounter is weak. It is the strong man who can commit himself totally to another even to the extent of losing rigid mastery over himself. By definition, ecstasy only occurs when we have "let go," when we have transcended ourselves, when we have lost control. The necessity of losing control is most obvious, of course, in married friendship. When a husband or wife are holding back their bodies in the act of love, the result for both of them is unsatisfying and disappointing. The ecstasy the act is designed to produce does not occur probably because the more generalized ecstasy of friendship in their marriage relationship is also deficient.

In friendship relationships that are not genital, physical ecstasy is obviously much more subdued than it is between married partners, but there is an ecstatic element in all friendship. Ecstasy, by definition, is a phenomenon of being drawn outside oneself, of "standing out" apart from the routines and systems of our everyday behavior. Friendship produces such an impact because it is the attractiveness and the support, the seduction and the encouragement of the friend that enables us to be ourselves, to break out of the ordinary barriers that constrict the self.

Friendship draws the self out. If there is no ecstasy, there is no friendship. The delight we experience may not be the psychedelic delight of blinding colors and pounding drums, but it need not be. Human ecstasy can take many forms. The most satisfying kind of ecstasy is that in which the self enjoys full consciousness of its goodness and its power of attracting the other and of responding to the other. We do not necessarily have to have sound and light, rock music and flashing colors. In the best of friendships the sound and the lights frequently just get in the way.

12

FRIENDSHIP AND FREEDOM

Friendship is the breaking out of a prison, a prison in which we feel very warm and comfortable because it is so familiar to us, a prison we hate to leave behind because we're not sure that we will find anything quite as good in the world outside. But we encounter in friendship a different kind of trap, a trap that we have freely chosen, a trap that oddly enough liberates us more and more. Friendship necessarily restricts our freedom. Just as he who chooses to go north is no longer free to go south, he who chooses to make a commitment to a friend is now not free to withdraw the commitment. Such a statement is a hard saying to devotees of pop psychology who seem to think that they can combine "doing your own thing," "total availability," and "absolute freedom." How you can be totally available and absolutely free at the same time, how you can do your own thing and be responsible to others at the same time is not immediately clear.

Consistency to one's commitments is a higher virtue than

total spontaneity. Freedom is a more admirable quality when it is focused and disciplined. Our freedom in a friendship is restricted by the ontological and existential demands of the relationship, but such restrictions make it a more admirable and more impressive and richer freedom than a freedom that feels weighted by no responsibility to the other (which, be it noted, is worlds apart from responsibility *for* the other).

In any friendship relationship we have the radical freedom to withdraw even though the exercise of such a freedom would be disastrously irresponsible. More painful is the realization that we must always respect the other's freedom to withdraw, however insistently we will protest his irresponsibility if he should do so. Freedom in friendship implies the possibility of the end of friendship, an anguish that is always involved in a relationship between friends, and that must be faced honestly unless we are to deceive ourselves about friendship.

But there are varying degrees of determination of friendship, just as there are varying levels of trust in the relationship between friends. The absolute termination of friendship means that the relationship is finished; but other friendships can survive, though at a diminished level of effectiveness and trust when initiatives to expand and deepen the friendship are rejected. In both instances, we must respect the freedom of the friend either to reject us partially or to reject us totally.

One of the most complicated skills required in friendship is the ability to recognize when one goes away with a demand so that one may return with it on another and better day. The trouble with a decision to temporarily suspend a demand is that the evidence on which such a decision must be based is generally very uncertain and ambiguous.

I think of a friend for whom I have great affection whom I have known since I taught her in sixth-grade gram-

mar school. Not so long ago, I rather dramatically mod-
ified the style of our relationship by demanding that she
face a certain aspect of her behavior that was severely im-
pairing the effectiveness of the contribution she was making
to the world. Needless to say, one takes a fairly serious risk
when one engages in such an endeavor. One expects that
the response will be ambivalent and, in this situation, the
ambivalence of the response was so dramatic as to baffle
me completely. In the four or five conversations we had
on the subject, I found myself almost literally with two
different persons. In the first part of the conversation she
was negative, mildly hostile, and quite confident that if the
problem had ever existed, and it probably hadn't, she had
it completely under control. Then, in the middle of the
conversation, dramatically and almost without warning, she
became a completely different person, crying and laughing,
smiling happily, and refusing to say a word. The incredible
thing was that each of our interviews proceeded along exactly the same path. It seemed to me that she was both
terrified of the subject I had raised and very happy that
it was at last out in the open.

Each conversation began with the blunt statement that
she absolutely did not want to talk about the subject any
more and would certainly not come back again, and then
the scenario would be replayed, but there was, after several
sessions, no modification of the scenario and no sign that
any movement or growth had taken place.

At this point, I found myself in a rather difficult position. I am not a psychotherapist and I do not even like
to mix pastoral counseling with friendship. To have pushed
any farther toward uncovering the roots of her problem and
the causes of her contradictory behavior would, my instincts
told me, be stepping beyond the bonds of friendship and
moving in the direction of therapy. I also heard my in-

stincts warning me that, at this stage in her life, a friend ought not to attempt any more for her than I had already attempted, and if I persisted in my demand, I might do a disservice both to her and to the friendship. Therefore, somewhat reluctantly, I pursued the matter no more and permitted her to act as though those very strange second halves of our conversations had never occurred. I made it as clear as I could that I still thought the problem was there, but also assured her that she would hear no more about it from me, at least at the present time.

The reader may think that I lack courage, and he may very well be right; at a younger age I think I would have plunged recklessly ahead, but it seems to me that at that particular interlude in my young friend's life, the best thing I could do for her would be to support her by respecting her freedom to insist that her unreality was real. I am not at ease with this decision, but I would be even more ill at ease with its opposite. Friendship, of course, demands honesty, but it doesn't dictate the time, the place, or the style of honesty. Sensitive and sophisticated friends, I think, are most discreet and diplomatic about waiting for the appropriate time. As we acquire a little bit more wisdom, we realize how many times are inappropriate, how frequently impulsiveness results from our own insecurities and anxieties and not from an objective evaluation of the needs of our friend.

The only trouble is that if we are too discreet and too prudent in waiting for the appropriate time, we will end up by discovering that the time has already passed.

It is thus part of friendship that we must be content with incompletenesses and imperfections and inadequacies in our friendships. We must be willing to accept the rejection of some of our initiatives and the abuse of some of our trust and the turning away from part of our invitation.

Such inadequacies do not necessarily destroy a friendship, nor even weaken it, though they certainly inhibit its growth. If the inadequacies and incompletenesses and rejections and the misunderstandings become pervasive, however, we are then faced with the second and more serious problem of friendship and freedom, the agonizing question of whether friendships can come to an end.

I have written a number of columns on friendship for the *National Catholic Reporter,* and after each one received letters from spouses who said they know exactly what I mean because they have been open and honest and trusting in the marriage relationship and their partner had rejected them, had responded to trust with suspicion, to openness with anger, and to love with rejection. It is clear from each letter that the writer felt that she was completely justified and that her husband had failed her. What she wanted, of course, was validation from me of her husband's guilt and her innocence. I am afraid she didn't get it.

There are relationships in which every possible initiative that one person can make is totally and categorically rejected by the other. Such relationships are few, I suspect, but they exist, and people who are trapped in them deserve our profound sympathy. But in most of those instances when someone devotes all of his attention to analyzing the faults of the other and seems quite unaware that he may have contributed a considerable amount of tension and strife to the relationship, I remain skeptical. Friendships do end, at least before a certain point of definitive commitment has been reached, and they even end because one person has rejected the other, but I am prepared to believe in the relative innocence of the rejectee only when that person shows an awareness of what he has contributed to the decline of the friendship. It is almost axiomatic that the one who is passionately eager to place the blame on the other probably must bear a good deal of the responsibility himself for what has happened to the friendship. The more you proclaim your innocence, the more I am persuaded of your guilt.

But why do friendships come to an end? The most obvious explanation is that two people involved in a relationship cannot or will not break out of their defense systems. Neither one is even remotely interested in taking actual risks or in making authentic efforts to overcome terror. The essential concern of both partners is to find justification for themselves and guilt for the other. In such circumstances the two people are adolescents at best and infants at worst, and they are not likely to be anything more for the rest of their lives—barring a miracle or psychotherapy or both. In such relationships, friendship was never really a serious issue.

The second set of circumstances at which friendship comes to an end exists when there may be some openness to possibilities of trust and delight, but the partners do not have enough electricity and enough seductiveness to make intimacy so powerfully enough attractive that it becomes irresistible. They may lack the attractiveness for one another because they do not share enough of the same life values and goals, enough of the same interests and commitments and expectations to provide the raw material for intimacy, or it may be that in the given state of both their emotional developments, mutual attractiveness is so effectively hidden that it will never have a chance to emerge. Such friendships, I think, will not end with recrimination or anger but will rather decline and vanish—unless it happens to be a marriage friendship, in which case the husband and wife have themselves a very neat problem.

The third variety of the breakup of a friendship is more tragic and more painful. The two people involved do indeed exercise strong attraction on one another. They have successfully seduced each other out of the comfortable prison of their fears. They have begun to experience delight in the midst of their terrors. They may be very close to the point of no return but they are also, alas, very frightened; so there is a rise in anger and vindictiveness, in scapegoating and projecting, in all the complicated unconscious tricks that we use to convert our friend into a replacement of a parent or a sibling. The search for blame and guilt becomes of paramount importance, and both partners resolutely refuse to acknowledge their own unconscious contribution to the strife and to analyze what mistakes they have made in the relationship. The other's guilt must be delineated and then acknowledged and confessed; only when that happens, only when the other one accepts blame for everything that has gone wrong, can the friendship get back on track. The possibility of the unconscious must be vigorously denied. It is inconceivable that one may have some unconscious investments in the strife and that one may be as much to blame as the other for the mess the two have jointly produced.

I am afraid that many friendships break up at just precisely this point. The two friends may depart with a spectacular outburst or, particularly if they are married, the friendship may sink back to a low level of satisfaction in which the relationship is sustained by inertia, periodically punctured by outbursts of passion or of anger. It is at this point in a relationship that the two friends desperately need the help of someone else, surely not an arbitrator to judge what is right, or even a mediator who will try to work out a compromise, but rather a sounding board who will enable them to see objectively what has been happening. The wise investor, however, will not put too much money on a successful outcome.

But there is a fourth way in which friendship comes

to an end, one whose possibility must be honestly faced even though it is the last explanation for the decline of a friendship that a partner in the friendship should fall back on. It may well be that no matter how seductive our invitation, no matter how complete our gift, no matter how total our promise, the other simply will not respond authentically. Under such circumstances, let it be very clear, we have no choice but to get out. There is necessarily an upper limit to how much frustration and rejection we can take without having our integrity and our self-respect collapse. A person who risks himself in a friendship after it has become clear that no matter what he does there will be no authentic response is taking an unjustifiable risk with his own personal validity. He may think he is strong enough not to get hurt, but he is kidding himself and, to use American slang, he'd better get out while the getting is good.

My own inclinations have led me to stay in frustrating relationships long after it should have been clear to me that there was not the remotest chance of authentic response. I had walked, as the Scripture says, the second, the third, and the fourth, and perhaps the hundreth mile, and I had walked much too far for my own good and for the good of the other. I cannot claim that I was innocent of mistake or neurosis, or of unconscious manipulation, which made bad matters worse. But it ought to have been clear to me that my own mistakes and unconscious drives were largely irrelevant. If I had made no mistakes, and if I had been the most mature and healthy of men, there would still have been no opportunity to break through the barriers of inauthenticity and distortion that were set up against me. Although I did not get out while the getting was good, I was forced to get out while the getting was bad, with notable suffering for all involved.

It is very difficult to resign oneself to rejection, especially when the issue is never perfectly clear—it never is in human relationships—and when one is all too well aware that one's own hands are anything but clean. Yet, once again, we must believe the most authentic and healthy of our instincts, and when these instincts say, "Get out," then we should get out just as quickly as we possibly can.

What is required in such situations is a total respect for the freedom of the other and a radical refusal to despair about the other. Only when we can have hope for him and respect his freedom are we able to resign ourselves to the fact that there is nothing more that we can do for the other without risking harm to ourself. It sounds so very calm and serene when it is put that way—"hope," "respect," "freedom," "nothing more that we can do." But in the existential situation, with the pain of rejection and the swirling currents of anger, with the consciousness of the hurt we have received and guilt about the hurt we have caused, the best we can hope for is an escape from disaster that leaves us with some shreds of our dignity and self-respect. Yet one does not recover from the termination of friendship the day after it happens.

Somehow or other, we should try to make clear when a friendship ends that we still hope for the possibility that it may begin again, that we will still endeavor to maintain a warm availability for the other. It is hard to communicate such a feeling of warmth and availability, especially when our strongest emotions are of relief and eagerness to get completely away from the foolish mess in which we have been caught. There isn't really much hope, though there is always some, that the future will hold any promise for renewed affection, particularly since we are the one who has terminated it, although the other has forced us into a situation where we have no choice. The ploy is a very clever one. We have been forced in desperation to end a relationship that we realize is destroying both of us, but the fact that we end it merely preserves the other's neurotic conviction that we have hated him all along, and there is absolutely nothing we can do to shake that conviction.

The possibility of such a trauma is inherent in every intimate human friendship. As we become wiser in the ways of the human personality, more sensitive to our own self, and more perceptive about the selfhood of others, the risks of such traumas decrease. We are more careful and more discreet about the kind of friendship relationships we begin. We become sophisticated about the sorts of personalities with whom we get involved. We know enough about ourselves to realize that there are, at least in the present state of the evolution of the species, a number of personality types with whom intimacy for us would never be possible. We learn how to choose our friends and thus substantially diminish the possibility of the end of friendship.

13

HOW TO CHOOSE A FRIEND

Friendship is choice, it is focusing our resources on one person rather than on another. It is a long series of decisions as to the next appropriate move in the dance. It is a determination to push on in the face of obstacles that strongly suggest that we should not push on. Friendship is the exercise of an option that at all times we are radically free not to exercise. It is a signal called on third down and three with the knowledge that all the Monday morning quarterbacks, particularly the one who works in our own mind, will judge us if we don't make the required yardage.

We don't like choice. We try to blur options so as to escape from choice. We try to force the external environment to make the decision. We attribute our choice to others. We do almost anything to escape the responsibility of having to make our own decision. The craze for computer dances, and even computer marriages, is merely a ludicrous caricature of man's escape from the dread of choice. If only we could make the computer be responsible for our destiny.

If only we did not have to live with the consequences of our decisions. If only we could escape the anxiety that comes from thinking that things could be very different and much better if we had made the opposite choice. If only we were strong enough to take responsibility for ourselves.

And yet, friendship is still choice. We cannot be completely rational in our decisions about friendship—indeed, we cannot be completely rational in almost all of our decisions—but neither is there any reason to be irrational. We do not calculate friendship mathematically, but neither do we turn over responsibility to our raw emotions. There is unquestionably an electricity between friends, a chemistry, an instinctual response that says, "Here friendship is possible." As we grow wiser and more experienced, we become more sophisticated about this instinct and realize when its chemistry and electricity are deceiving us. We are able to distinguish between the instant rapport that is authentic and that which is deceptive and dangerous. We should never completely distrust our instincts, but we should never completely trust them either.

If there is something of the instinctive in the friendship, however, there must also be something of the rational. Our friendship will not survive crisis unless we have in common with one another values and interests and goals. If we have nothing to talk about with our friend, then there is not going to be much point in the friendship. We should be able to discuss the problems in our relationship with calmness and objectivity and wit; there should be a general smoothness in our friendship, a lack of dramatic ups and downs in most circumstances. We should be able to work together, to count on one another to be responsible and reliable in our common work. We should, above all, be able to play together, to let ourselves go in fun and frolic without feeling awkward or embarrassed or ill at ease. If, on the contrary, in playful situations we find ourselves withdrawing from the friend, then the warning sign is set right in the middle of the highway.

Somewhere between instincts and reason is the "feel" of friendship, the awareness of the full personality, that a relationship is enriching us and developing us, causing our goodness to expand, and making us more ourselves. To what extent does the friendship lead us to more anger and self-punishment, or does it rather help us to become more satisfied with ourselves, more respectful of our own dignity and validity? How much peace and joy does it bring us or, on the contrary, does it make us jumpy and anxious? How much does this friendship enable us to be tolerant of others beyond the relationship? How much ease does it put into our rapport with the physical and social environment in which we find ourselves? Does it enable us to see ourselves more clearly or, on the contrary, has the reality of self become more obscure? Does the relationship "feel" good or does it "feel" bad?

It has often seemed to me unfortunate that young people make the choice of their most intimate friend long before they are able to ask any of the above questions or at least to ask them sensitively and intelligently. Perhaps as the human race evolves further we will develop techniques for training our young people in wisdom about friendship choice before they have to make the critical choice of the marriage partner; whenever that evolutionary phase arrives there will certainly be far more friendship in the world than there is at the present time.

In our society the choice of a friend is especially difficult for the very weak and for the very strong. The weak, those whose confidence in themselves is almost nonexistent, look for a friend who will compensate for their weakness and frequently end up with a replica of the parent who made them weak in the first place. A person who expects to find the strength and validity that he thinks he completely lacks himself is courting disaster. Such a person should be advised to stay away from friends whom he admires for their strength. Such strength is often illusory and covers up for weakness not unlike that which harasses the person who feels his own weakness. On the contrary, a person who thinks he is weak should seek for friendship someone for whom weakness or strength don't seem to be important issues. In such a relationship he may discover himself that weakness is an irrelevant question.

The more difficult and more subtle problem is the one that faces the talented person. In our highly competitive society the talented person is likely to be chipped away at from the very beginning of his life. Even though we have a meritocracy, more or less, in which talent is awarded financially and economically, we have a competitive meritocracy where the unfair advantage of the gifted person is deeply resented. I've often felt very sorry for the gifted children whom I see in school (in part because I guess I was a gifted child, though heaven knows I didn't know that). It's bad enough if their parents had chosen to make a big display of their precociousness, but it is far worse if the parents are determined—as are so many middle-class parents—to cut the gifted child down to size lest he threaten his brothers and sisters and, if the truth be told, his parents, too. His classmates in school resent him—he knows too much, his marks are too high, he always has the answers, he even corrects the teacher's mistakes, it is not fair for him to get things so effortlessly. Who does he think he is, anyhow? His teachers from kindergarten to graduate school are also made uneasy by him because he seems to know more than they do. No teacher likes to be reminded by a student of his own feelings of inferiority. And in the occupational world his colleagues will resent his brilliance and his flair, his ability to do things quickly and well when they must work long and hard to dsplay half as much competence as he does. Would-be friends may flock around him to bask in the reflected light of his glory, but he should beware of such friends, for they secretly envy and hate him and would, if they could, drag him down to their own levels.

If he survives to adulthood with some sense of his own worth and value, then he must be careful to become involved in intimate relationships only with those who are not threatened by him. If the harassment that has marked his childhood and adolescence has deprived him of his self-confidence, he is in deep trouble. Despite all his immense strengths and gifts he will have no faith in himself, no awareness of his own value and dignity. The vultures will swirl around him ready to pounce on him, his friends will be eager to cut him down to their size, and he will find himself defenseless against such assaults. He will simply not be able to understand how someone who is as weak as he is can be viewed as strong by others, nor how someone as defenseless and fragile as he is can be so viciously attacked by those whom he thought were his friends. He may find himself devoutly wishing he was like everyone else but, alas for him and our competitive technocracy, he is not like everyone else. He may as well resign himself to a life in which he will be greatly rewarded by viciously hated.

The gifted person does not have to have friends as gifted as he. What he needs, rather, are friends who are strong enough to enjoy his gifts without being threatened by them. Strong enough to have loved him for what he is without having to try to cut him down to size, gentle enough to heal his wounds when his enemies yap at his heels, tender enough to caress him out of his moods when he is depressed and discouraged by the animosity of others which, try as he might, he simply cannot understand, and resourceful enough to persuade him that he is indeed lovable, not merely despite his gifts but, in fact, because of them. The giant on the mountaintop looks so mighty and powerful that one would conclude that he does not need friends. In fact, he needs them more than others, or the mountaintop will turn into a wall and he will become humpty-dumpty, and the king's horses with the king's men will arrive to support him just a little bit too late.

But all of us, the weak, the gifted, the ordinary (although no one is ordinary) must have friends if we wish to be human. We must choose; we must decide which one of those frightening, terrifying "others" in the world outside we are going to entrust ourselves to. It's a hard choice to make. We'd rather not make it, and yet some of the others seem so attractive, so irresistible, that we know we have to choose; and so, decide we do, with fear and trepidation, but also with the beginning of trust, with hesitant faith in our instincts as well as the beginning of shrewd calculations. As Mr. Dooley remarked in the motto of this volume, "Trust ihvryone, Hinnissey, but make sure the cards are cut."

14

FRIENDSHIP AND PATIENCE

In the previous chapters of this book I have described friendship in a somewhat static context, as though the two poles of trust and distrust were adjacent to one another and one could cross from distrust to trust in one quick, dramatic move.

There are, certainly, dramatic turning points in the friendship relationship, times of great transitional crises, when a friendship either moves ahead rapidly to a new kind of joy and delight or when it begins to fall apart. There are no automatic but certain resolutions of such crises. Two friends who have been quite close to one another may resolve such crises either by traumatically terminating their friendship or by beginning to drift apart.

But if there are decisive turning points in any friendship, it does not therefore follow that progress in friendship is rapid. In many cases, movement between the dramatic leaps can be agonizingly slow, almost so slow as to be invisible. The moments of glory are preceded and followed by moments of hesitant and painful growth; if we are not prepared to endure the pain and the hesitancy of such slow growth then we are not very well equipped to play the friendship game.

Friendship is a relearning process. We have learned distrust and suspicion, and now we must unlearn them and acquire the skills of hopefulness and self-revelation. Since we have spent most of our lives learning how to fear, we cannot expect that we will learn how to love overnight, nor can we expect this of our friends.

The example of a wife who is learning how to be sexually responsive is a classic case in point. One can assume that she wants to learn, partly because of duty, partly because of curiosity, and partly because there are fires of passion smoldering at some level in her personality. But she has learned to distrust her womanhood, to be suspicious of pleasure, to be afraid of men, and to try to control every situation with a man by keeping him off balance. She cannot be sexually responsive unless she learns how to surrender, but nothing in her life has prepared her to surrender, and much has taught her to avoid surrender at all costs. Even with much sincerity and good will she will acquire skills of surrender only slowly and awkwardly. Her husband cannot force the process. He must, of course, insist on growth, but he must be patient when the growth is sometimes quite slow. He must be wary of the tricks that she unconsciously plays, tempting him either to give up or to demand too much too soon. He must not let her threaten his masculinity, because if she succeeds in doing this he will lose either his patience or his firmness and, perhaps eventually, both.

The husband—or, indeed, any friend who is trying to break through barriers of suspicion or distrust—must have a great deal of faith and confidence, both in himself and in the other. Sometimes his faith and confidence must be sustained through periods of weariness, when it seems as if there never will be any change. It is not hard to be patient when there is evidence that patience is a successful strategy, but patience only becomes virtue when it doesn't seem to be working. Paradoxically enough, it is precisely this kind of patience that is most likely to be successful.

One friendship in which I have been involved had been most painful and frustrating for months and even years. Try as I might, I was not able to escape from the distortion and misinterpretation that this friend insisted on pursuing. I was the complete father-figure, and her defenses were so systematic that there was no way of escaping from the father-figure prison that she had created for me. After many months of fruitlessly trying, there was one more long, foolish, painful conversation. After she and her husband had left, I resolved that I wanted no more of it, that the friendship was too frustrating to be worth the effort, and I was going to get out as quickly as I could. When she phoned two days later, I was fully prepared to suggest that she look elsewhere for a priest. Indeed, I almost began by saying just that (how splendid that would have been of me!) but, before I could, she began to speak in a tone of voice completely different from what I had heard for a long time. Before the first three sentences were out of her mouth, it was clear that the father-figure was dead. I wish I could claim credit for having handled that particular problem with skill and intelligence. My patience, I fear, was much less than it should have been through the whole conflict, but the point is that I almost blew it just a few seconds before victory because I was not quite patient enough.

To have patience, then, we first of all must have confidence. As confidence decreases, impatience increases. When we find ourselves angry, harassed, worried, threatened, insecure, we lash out against others in angry defense of ourselves. The husband will become impatient with his wife on a day when he has been harassed in his job quite independently of anything his wife has said or done. In fact, on his way home from work he has made up his mind (however unconsciously) that he is going to take out his frustrations on his wife. What he does not realize is that he is afraid to risk his masculinity, badly injured on the job, with a woman who might reject it. His impatience is a defense against her challenge to him. If her day has led her to doubt her own worth as a woman, and she feels the need to throw up the barrier of impatience to protect her fragile femininity from masculine challenge, the evening and the night are very likely to be disasters. The two bodies may be close to one another, but the invisible walls that have been built up because of fear of primordial inadequacy keep the two personalities far apart even if the bodies are temporarily and unsatisfactorily linked.

Note well what has happened: The failures and harassments of the day at work have called into question his success in his career. His masculinity is threatened, his confidence impeded. He does not feel adequate to cope with his wife. She, on the other hand, feels that she has not performed well at that which validates her—the role of housewife and mother—so her confidence and ability to relate to her husband are impaired. Impatience and anger are "coverups" for feelings of inadequacy and incompetence. Only the very confident person can afford to dispense with the opaque garb of patience.

The very insecure and threatened person must have instantaneous change, either in other people or in society. He who demands instant success has a very tenuous grasp on his own selfhood—and, indeed, a very tenuous grasp on history, sociology, and psychology, too. For human wisdom tells us that all change is necessarily gradual. There may be times of dramatic progress, but they are prepared for and followed by times when the pace of change and growth is far more pedestrian.

The more difficult aspect of patience in friendship is determining when and how to "push" our friend. When do we make demands? How should the demands be made? When should we remain silent? How long should we wait before speaking out? When have we spoken too much? And when have we said too little? When have we come on too strong? And when have we come on too weak? When has our seductiveness been too powerful and has frightened the other away? And when has it been not powerful enough and hence not encouraged him enough?

It is so difficult to interpret the code, for sometimes the other's slowness and silence are pleas for challenge and encouragement, and at other times they are pleas that he be given a bit of breathing space. Even with all the confidence in the world, it is still so easy to make a mistake, to misread the signs completely. I suspect that more mistakes are made by not "pushing" hard enough than are made by "pushing" too hard or, to put the matter differently, more mistakes are made by being less seductive than are made by being too seductive. More mistakes are made be equating patience with inaction than by equating it with firm and vigorous demands. Most of the mistakes that are made in friendship are made by giving up too soon, though surely some are made by giving up far too late.

Our language remains inadequate to deal with the complexities of the friendship relationship because the process we have described in the previous paragraphs as proceeding in one direction is generally an interaction process. Both friends are making demands on each other; both are challenging each other; both are trying to practice confidence and creative patience with each other. Each one is trying to be patient with the other's impatience and to plead with the other to be patient with his own impatience. The wife who is learning from the husband how to be a successful female lover is, in the process, teaching him how to be a successful male lover. He teaches her the meaning of femininity and she teaches him the meaning of masculinity; he, by becoming more of a male and she, by becoming more of a woman. Their passion and love force them to be impatient, but their tenderness and concern moderate the impatience with confident patience. There is no more difficult skill in the friendship game than that which is required to exercise a patience that demands neither too much nor too little and that yields all it can without attempting to yield more than it can.

One of the strongest supports of patience is an awareness that friendship grows richer through effort. As we look back on the important moments of friendship, we discover that they are not the moments when there is no strain or conflict, but rather the moments when we and our friend overcame difficulties and problems together. Patience has no greater enemy than that shallow romanticism that lacks tolerance for ambiguity and uncertainty. Human relationships have a permanently happy ending only on the movie or TV screen. Friendships in which all problems are surmounted at one time exist only in the most dramatic novels, not in the real world in which we are forced to live. He who permits himself to be disillusioned when he discovers that both he and his friend have much to learn about the skills of the friendship game should not have gotten in the game in the first place. A romanticism that is disappointed when we do not "live happily ever after" is a romanticism that has not matured beyond the level of the nursery rhyme.

Patience is reinforced when we are experiencing pay-offs in other dimensions of our life. Just as the man who has lost confidence on his job also loses confidence in his ability to obtain response from his wife, so a man who permits himself to be satisfied with his performance on his job will be a much more clever and skillful lover for his wife. No human friendship should be made to bear the burden of providing all the happiness in our lives. As my colleague, Norman Bradburn, has ably demonstrated, happiness is not the absence of strife or conflict but, rather, a favorable "balance of payments" between happiness and unhappiness. To put the matter in economic terms, which may seem a bit harsh, the only way we can be certain of happiness in life is to diversify our emotional investments. Not only does such diversification enhance the probability of a favorable balance of payments, it also gives us the strength and confidence we need to deal with a relationship that is not working out quite as well as we would like to see it. If we have but one friendship, then that friendship is in grave jeopardy. If we have many friendships, of which one has some troubles, we have a great deal more confidence in our ability to solve the problems and a great deal more patience with the sufferings, loneliness, and fear of the other.

In a society where professional success is as important to man as it is in our society, it is not surprising that many men must achieve some sort of confidence in their professional ability before they are secure enough or patient enough to be good friends or good lovers. Some men, of course, are so shaken by fear and anxiety that there is no success great enough to give them confidence. Each new success, then, demands yet greater achievement and draws them away from their friends and family instead of giving them the security and confidence they need in their masculinity to become good husbands and good friends; but for many other men, the sweet smell of professional success makes them far richer friends and far more competent lovers. Unfortunately, there is no similar way in which a woman can taste success in those things that presumably validate her as a woman. Even if she happens to be good in some professional area, she has not been made to think that this kind of skill confirms her femininity. Income and occupational rank validate her husband's masculinity, but it's much less clear as to what is required to be a woman and much more difficult to measure how feminine one is. I'm not sure exactly what the solution to this problem might be, though it is hard to escape the conclusion that we do a much poorer job of training girls and young women in self-respect and confidence than we do in training boys and young men.

In the present state of the friendship game, however, one must conclude that a man will have his masculinity confirmed both by his career and by his woman, while a woman will have her femininity confirmed only by her man, if at all. The necessity for a man to realize how important he is in assuring his woman that she is a woman is, one fears, not understood by most men.

If our validity as men and women are to be confirmed partially or totally by the opposite sex, does it follow that only the spouse can provide such confirmation, or can it be provided by others besides the spouse and, on occasion, by others instead of the spouse? A number of comments are appropriate on this somewhat delicate and difficult question:

From what we said in the previous paragraphs about the risk of putting all of one's emotional investments in one relationship, it would follow that the confirmations of our value as men and women ought to come from many different people and in many different ways. We cannot expect to have the necessary patience for dealing with a critical relationship if that relationship is the only one that validates us.

For married people, the most important confirming relationship is obviously the one with the spouse. If we are not accepted as a man or a woman at the supper table or in the bedroom, then we are going to have a rather difficult time in other contexts of our life.

Nevertheless, if we permit ourselves to be man or woman only for our spouse, then the marriage will be subjected to severe pressures. The fact that we are able to be man or woman for our spouse should make it possible for us to be man or woman with anyone with whom we deal. Similarly, if we permit ourselves to see our validity as male or female reflected by those to whom we are not married, then we will be that much more of a man or a woman for the lover to whom we are married.

The question of whether other relationships can contribute a validation that a given marriage does not, without the marriage promises being violated, is an extraordinarily difficult one for which at the present time there are no easy answers. Can a man have "another woman" in his life to confirm his masculinity while that woman with whom he does have marital intercourse ignores, if she does not impede his masculinity? Can a woman find fulfillment in a friendship with another man while at the same time being faithful to a husband who has lost interest or, more likely, never was interested in her as a woman? The romantic answer to both of these questions is "Yes." A more realistic answer, I think, would indicate a good deal of skepticism and reserve. Such relationships may be possible but they are not easy, and most of those who think they have wisely entered into such relationships are only kidding themselves, either because they have not given the marriage an honest try or because they lack the maturity and the self-possession to carry off either a genital or a platonic outside relationship.

Patience, then, requires that we be confident in ourselves, that we understand that patience ultimately enhances the rewards of the friendship game, and that we diversify our emotional investments. It also requires, finally, that we really desire our friend; if we are going through the motions of patience and do not expect that should our patience be rewarded the payoff will be very great, we are being fair neither to ourselves nor to the other. The tired, weary patience that marks so many family gatherings at Thanksgiving and Christmas is a ritual that is not based on hope for an improvement in the relationship. There is no expectation that an improvement would make much difference. This book is scarcely the place to deal with the Thanksgiving and Christmas syndrome, but the inauthentic and forced patience of these two horrendous festivals is not the kind of patience that makes friendship possible. We can be really patient only with somebody whom we really want. Married lovers are patient with each other's fumbling inadequacies because they delight in each other despite the inadequacies and because they believe that because the inadequacies decrease, delight will become even more spectacular. Patience without desire and without delight is a sterile and deadly patience.

And, oh yes, there is one final reason for being patient with others, and it may be the most powerful reason of all: They are being patient with us, and they are finding it every bit as difficult to be patient with us as we find it to be patient with them. We are going to make it, my friend and I, we are going to be patient enough with ourselves and with each other to overcome the angry self-defense of impatience—but usually only by the skin of our teeth.

15

FRIENDSHIP AND TENDERNESS

Patience, however, is not enough. It is essentially a passive and negative dimension of the relationship. It means we do not give up, we do not moderate our demands, we do not punish the other for not being instantaneously responsive. Unless patience is blended with another virtue, it can become sterile, indifferent, and even haughty and supercilious. The name of that other virtue is tenderness.

Tenderness is the ability to create for our friend an atmosphere of warmth that is first of all a physical gentleness rooted in concern for the other and a realization of our own immense power over the other. In the most primordial and basic sense we have the power to hurt others, we have the potential of causing physical pain to others; the other, in his primordial fears, knows that we have the ability to inflict pain upon him. In a very profound and radical sense, fear of physical pain is involved in all human relationships. A child is afraid the parent will hurt him. The wife is afraid her husband will injure her. The husband is not sure whether the wife's fear of him is so great that she may do him injury as a means of self-defense. It is part of the paradox of the human condition that we must be aggressive if we are to establish relations with one another, but that aggressiveness is almost certain to create terror in the other. Tenderness is the protective coating that we put around our aggressiveness to assure the other that while indeed we want to possess him, the last thing we want to do is to hurt him in our act of possession. A husband is physically gentle with his wife because his caresses reassure her that she will not be hurt, and she caresses him in response so that he may know that his aggressiveness is understood and that she does not feel the need to punish him before he hurts her.

But the basic and primordial physical tenderness between husband and wife is merely a paradigm for a larger, more important, and more pervasive psychological tenderness that must characterize the relationship not only between married lovers but between all friends. If there is not psychological tenderness in a marriage then physical tenderness will be meaningless and cannot be sustained. And if there is not psychological tenderness then no human friendship can long endure. Unless we are able to create an atmosphere of warmth in which our friend is assured he has no need to fear us, then he will not let us get close to him. When we try to do so he will turn and run.

The need for tenderness is grounded in the vulnerability and fragility of human nature. Man hurts easily. Unlike the rhinoceros, he has no armor plate and, unlike some other animals, he lacks thick skin. Quite the contrary, in fact; man is both physically and psychologically vulnerable. He hurts easily, and he is able to survive only because of his intelligence and wit. But his intelligence and wit make him far more suspicious than most animals. He becomes good at running either physically or psychologically because he has to be. Man keeps his defenses up because the environment in which he finds himself is threatening, particularly when that environment is peopled by other human beings. Man knows from his past experience that some of those other human beings would like to hurt him if they could. If others get too close to his piece of turf then he becomes very defensive because he is not sure what they are going to do to him. Friendship means that man lets others onto his turf, first physically and then psychologically, that he lowers his defenses, that he permits himself to be vulnerable, that he lets the other see his fragility and even gives him the opportunity to take advantage of that fragility. If the other does not show signs of reassurance—signs of reassurance that we've come to call tenderness—then the defenses will quickly go up again. We are giving the other the opportunity to wound us and destroy us. He had better reassure us that he does not intend to do harm or our suspicion and distrust will promptly return.

Sensitive, affectionate, gentle, sympathetic concern is what tenderness is all about. It is impossible for there to be too much of this quality in any human relationship. Man's capacity for fear and suspicion is almost without limit, and hence his capacity to lap up tenderness is also practically infinite. We sometimes laugh at our canine friends because they are so hungry for affection from their masters, but a dog's capacity for tenderness is quite small compared to his master's need and capacity for affection. The master may be just a bit more skillful at hiding it, but that means that he is really more suspicious and more frightened than his dog.

But there is more to tenderness. We acknowledge to our friend our vulnerability and fragility not only toward him but also toward the rest of the world. When he shows signs that he wishes to be tender and protective of us we are drawn toward putting ourselves in his hands so that he will protect us from those other suspicious and hostile foes who are lurking

145

just beyond the boundaries of our turf. If he really means what he says when he says that he does not intend to hurt us, then he will protect us from the others who seem inclined to do us in. If we have revealed to our tender friend how defenseless we really are then he simply has to respond by protecting us.

When a wife gives her body to her husband she cannot help but reveal to him the terror that this "letting go" of her self-possession involves. She may look forward eagerly to the delight, and yet her vulnerability in the love-making situation is so total and so pervasive, her surrender is so complete and so primordial, that she can make her gift only if there is the promise that he will receive the gift, will treasure it, and protect her from injury either by him or by others.

A man may seem less fragile and vulnerable in the act of seducing his wife, and yet he is perhaps more fragile and the risk he takes with himself is even greater than his wife has taken; she can demolish his confidence in his masculinity far more quickly than he can demolish her confidence in her femininity. Unless she is very sensitive to the fears involved in the risk he takes and is very gentle and tender in response to those fears, the terror for him will be even greater than it is for her. But once the married lovers have revealed to one another how fragile and vulnerable they are, how desperately they need the warmth that only tenderness can produce, then it is a short and inevitable step to expecting that the other's tenderness will not only guarantee that he will not hurt us but also guarantee that he will protect our fragility from assault by others. A husband who has cast caution to the winds to express his passionate devotion to his wife has revealed to her how weak and frightened he is, how much he needs her tenderness to function in the world beyond their relationship; and the wife who has abandoned all her restraints in order that she might passionately respond to her husband has revealed to him the nearly paralyzing terror that she had to overcome to make such a spectacular response. Having given herself completely over to his hands, she will now rely on him to protect her from anything else that might frighten her. For both of them, tenderness is an activity that once begun can never be ended.

As we have said so many times before, marriage is but the paradigm for all other relationships. Self-revelation to our friend requires tenderness as a response, and tenderness, in its turn, guarantees not only the affection of our friend but also his willingness to stand by us against all those who threaten us—or even, in some instances, to stand by us while we explore the possibility that perhaps some of those others lurking out there on the boundary of our turf might also want to be friends.

Tenderness, then, warms both the giver and the receiver; it is good to be able to rely on a powerful person and good to have someone else who sees us as a powerful person on whom he wishes to rely. Mutual tenderness acknowledges both our weakness and our power; to feel weak in the possession of another and to be powerful enough to possess another are both exhilarating, not to say ecstatic experiences. The tenderness rhythm is similar to the rhythm between the conquest and surrender we discussed in a previous chapter. Indeed, the power and weakness rhythm is a necessary prelude to the conquest and surrender rhythm, for we are only willing to surrender to someone who is powerful enough to protect us and we are only willing to run the risk of conquering someone who seems weak enough to need and accept and delight in our tenderness. In the final analysis, there is no more powerful means of seduction than to persuade the one we want to seduce that what we desperately need and want is tenderness.

Tenderness presupposes sensitivity. A tender person is

skilled at the art of introjection, which is merely a psycho-analytical way of saying that a tender person is able to "get inside" the other person and see the world from his view-point and to feel his fears from his viewpoint. The person who is good at introjection is the one who is confident enough to pay attention to the other in the relationship; he is secure enough in his own position to be able to take his attention off himself and focus it part of the time on the other, and he does not need to exhaust his energies wondering what the other thinks of him. He is enabled to devote some of his energies trying to understand what the other thinks of him-self and fears about himself. One need only look at some of our more narcissistic student radicals on television to realize that the human race still has a fair amount of evolutionary prog-ress ahead of it before it gets very good at seeing things from the viewpoint of someone else.

Tenderness is particularly good across sexual lines. Even though sympathy and tenderness between human beings are ultimately psychological rather than physical, they still have powerful physical roots. There is a certain chemistry of physi-cal and psychological in the relationship between the sexes that becomes almost an alchemy when it comes to under-standing and soothing someone else's fears. However, here one must concede that, as in so many other things, women are superior to men. Tenderness to a woman comes relatively easy. She can be tender not only with a man—and especially with her man—but also with other women. Men can be very tender with their own woman and, on occasion at least, tender with other women, though in both cases, the male's capacity for blundering insensitivities staggers the imagination, but it is a very rare man who is capable of being tender with other men. If tenderness is rooted in self-confidence—and it obviously is—one is therefore forced to conclude that women are far more self-confident than men. Perhaps the reason society has arranged more definite means for self-validation for men (as we discussed in the previous chapter) is that men need it more than women. If it is only the very self-confident man who is able to excel at tenderness with women, it is only a paragon of self-confidence who would take the grave risk of being tender with other men. Once again, we see persuasive evidence that the evolutionary progress of the race has a long way to go.

16

FRIENDSHIP AND SOCIETY

Friendship and love produce joy and happiness that are ecstatic, but part of the ecstasy is necessarily secret. The effects of friendship happiness are felt all around, and most observers are able to surmise the causes of the festivity of the friendship. And yet there are secrets between lovers (or among lovers, if one has groups of friends) that no one outside the relationship will be told, or indeed could be told. Only a husband knows how his wife looks and acts when they are making love, and only a wife is aware of her husband's strengths and skills as a lover. Even if they are on occasion unfaithful, the infidelity occurs in a transitory and artificial circumstance in which the person cannot be himself nearly as fully as he could be in love-making in a happy marriage. And even if others—such as doctors—have inspected the body of a man or a woman, they still cannot know what that body is like when challenged to its ultimate capacity for the giving and receiving of pleasure.

Husband and wife, therefore, possess the secret of each

other's body, and this secret is the focus around which many other secrets of their common existence are organized. No one else could possibly understand the subtle rhythm of their life together, the mistakes and blunders they have made in their relationship, the jokes that amuse only them, the fears that they have outgrown together, and the other fears with which they are still struggling. Such things are secret, in part because they are too private to be revealed to others, but in part also because others simply could not understand them. So, in many married friendships, shared secrets are an important part of the glue that holds the two friends together. Only a friend knows how good the other really is, and only the other knows how good the friend really is.

The friendship game is learned only by practice. In acquiring the skills of the game, friends make all kinds of mistakes, mistakes that become tragic unless they are treated as comedy. The blunders the bride and groom make as they attempt to understand the secrets of one another's body would absolutely destroy their relationship unless the two of them were capable of laughing at their awkwardness and inexperience. In any friendship there is awkwardness, misunderstanding, confusion, incongruity, and comedy, but always comedy that we would not dream of telling anyone else and that they probably would not understand if we did.

But there is another side of the story. Although it is surely true that the power of the secret is lost if it is more than hinted at to others around, it is also true that it must be hinted at. A husband and wife can do more than hint at their secret love and the subtle and not-so-subtle delights of that love, but they must hint at it. The secret of their love is too good to tell, but it's also too good to keep a complete secret. Indeed, the children who result from their love are a hint—though a fairly powerful hint—as to what goes on between the two of them. The joy of friendship must overflow the relationship between the friends. The child is a manifestation of the joy of the relationship between husband and wife although by no means the only, nor even an absolutely necessary manifestation of their love.

The joy of their love, the joy of their friendship must overflow. If it is pent up it will wither or, to put the matter somewhat more specifically, the joy of authentic friendship cannot be kept to the two friends. If they are successful in keeping the secret of the relationship totally to themselves, one is forced to conclude that their relationship is not authentic friendship. Man's capacity for happiness is infinite both in giving and in getting. Once he experiences joy in the highest form of human relationship—friendship—he must share this joy with others. Paul Claudel was right when he said that in love two people do not look so much at each other as they look together in the same direction, but he was right for ontological and psychological, rather than ethical reasons. It is not a question of friends expressing their gratitude to the universe for the joy of friendship by trying to bring happiness to others. Rather, the confidence and faith in themselves, the happiness that self-possession has brought to them, the secret that they have discovered must be communicated to others because confidence, joy, and ecstasy, by their very natures, cannot be concealed.

To put the matter from a somewhat different viewpoint, one of the critical problems in society is the absence of trust. Men cannot trust because they do not have enough friendship in their life. If there were more friendships in the world there would be more trust, and the level of tension in societal relations would decrease almost automatically. I am certainly not naïve enough to think that all efforts at social reform should be focused on improving the quality of friendships. The improvement of larger social structures cannot wait for the perfection of individual relationships, nor would the improvement of the individual relationships lead to the reform of the structure of society without drastic modifications of existing structures. Friendship is not a panacea, but it is a prerequisite, and in three senses:

Unless there is an increase in the quantity and quality of friendship, reformed social structures quickly are contaminated by new problems at least as bad as those eliminated by the reform.

If those who are the leaders of the reform movements do not have possession of their own selfhood, their own value, worth, and dignity that is rooted in their friendship relationships, then their crusades for social reform become means to an end not of improving human life but of validating their own worth. Such crusaders are but a step away from fanaticism.

To solve the kinds of problems of prejudice, war, and pollution that face the world today, we may well need a new kind of human being, a human being whose strength and confidence are rooted in a strong, supporting network of friendship and who is able both to trust others and to radiate trust among those with whom he interacts.

Friendship, then, may not reform society, but it is doubtful if society will be reformed adequately without friendship or that, if it is reformed, it will stay reformed unless there is far more love in the world than there is at the present time.

But there is yet another reason why friendship requires society: Friendship cannot be pursued as an end in itself.

Since this book is about friendship, it has analyzed directly the intricacies of the friendship game, but if two people set out to develop a friendship explicitly and consciously, they are very likely to fail. Friendship results not from direct effort but, rather, from shared experiences. Friendship is a by-product of common effort and not the direct result of that effort. Even in a friendship in marriage, where conscious and explicit concerns about improving the quality of the friendship are not only healthy but necessary, the love between the two partners is the result of their efforts to solve common problems and to see common goals, rather than direct attempts to modify the quality of their relationship.

There are times, of course, when a friendship must be highly self-conscious, but if self-consciousness pervades the relationship it very easily becomes artificial, convoluted, and stilted. We work out our relationships with our friend while we are busy doing things together. If we put off doing things together until we solve the problems of our friendship, then we will find ourselves caught in a very sticky quagmire or, to modify the metaphor, a self-conscious pursuit of the joy of friendship is like chasing a will-o'-the-wisp. It always just barely eludes us.

Friendship cannot be forced, cannot be pursued; it must flow rather from an interaction of common effort and common reflection, common play and common work, common joy and common sorrows, common honesty and common fears, common pleasure and common suffering. A friendship couple that turns in upon itself and tries to exclude from its relationship anything that does not pertain to the immediate issue of friendship will find itself in a very rarified atmosphere and will quickly discover that it is no longer even on the planet earth. It has found a landscape much like that of the moon, where there is no life and where even its own life is supported by most artificial means.

Can our friendship become a society? In most of the pages of this book I have discussed friendship as though it were a dyad, but it is possible for a friendship relationship to include more than two people, though we know very little about intimate friendships beyond the dyad level. There is some human wisdom from poetry, philosophy, religion, and the social sciences that helps us to understand the dyadic friendship but, beyond the dyad, our understanding is extraordinarily thin.

There have been in the past "bands of brothers," and in our own day we see the resurgent commune movement attempting to establish friendship communities despite the clear historical evidence that most such communities in the past have failed. One must applaud the enthusiasm and the courage of the pioneers of the new communes, though one has reservations about their wisdom for, if dyadic friendship is difficult to maintain, a multiple friendship relationship is far more complex. It can be done, it has been done, but it does not happen automatically, and it surely cannot be brought into being by putting a notice on a college bulletin board announcing that a commune is being convened.

One can take it that it is almost axiomatic that those who are naïve about the prospects of commune experiments are doomed to failure, for only those who realize the complexities of expanding a friendship beyond the dyad have much chance of success. Nonetheless, the frivolities and the naïveté of the commune movement should not be permitted to obscure the fact that the desire for friendship communities is an extraordinarily important cultural event.

Closely related to the communal movement is the attempt to achieve instant openness or instant trust through various gimmicks of group dynamics such as sensitivity training, encounter groups, marathon experiences and, more recently, such bizarre phenomena as "group groping" and "nude encounters." I would not want, of course, to deny that tremendous progress has been made in understanding the dynamics of human groups, nor would I even want to exclude on a priori grounds the possibility that some circumstances touching, embracing—and perhaps even nudity —may facilitate growth and friendship, but it does seem necessary to point out that gimmicks cannot create friendship and can frequently, on the contrary, stand in its way. Instant openness and instant trust are usually phony openness and phony trust.

But whatever the weaknesses and mistakes of both the commune movement and the group dynamics cult, the enthusiasm for them both indicates how powerful is this quest for friendship in our technological society. It may even turn out that many dyadic relationships can only prosper in an atmosphere of trust and affection that is generated by a larger friendship community.

I do not feel qualified to interpret the implications of my reflections on friendship in this book for friendship communities involving more than two persons. I must leave it to those readers who have experienced such groups to deduce for themselves what the implications of my comments are, if any, for the multiple friendship group. But there is one implication, at least, that I would like to draw to the reader's attention: We must, I think, be very skeptical of the sexual communitarians that some enthusiasts are advocating as the wave of the future—as though no one had ever thought of this in the past (they might want, for example, to consult the Koran).

Modern enthusiasts for sexual communitarians—such as the author of *The Harrad Experiment**—would persuade us that if we could once break out of the moral shackles that an obscurantist past has imposed upon us we can have happy, vigorous communities in which everyone sleeps with everyone else. There is a certain unconscious snobbery about the argument, as there is indeed about all of those who proclaim that they have broken with the moral narrowness of the past. To see oneself as the hinge of history, the first en-

* Robert H. Rimmer, *The Harrad Experiment*. Los Angeles: Sherbourne (1966).

lightened generation after countless generations of frightened obscurantists, is an heroic assumption, but it may also be a presumptuous one. Others, in bygone years, have thought that they were the first of the new generation only to discover that they, too, quickly became old-fashioned. I have no desire to be cast as a defender of rigid morality. Moral systems deteriorate rapidly from insight to legalistic ritualism, but it is snobbery to assume that there has been no wisdom in the past and that the moral systems we have inherited from the past do not contain within their legalisms and ritualisms a good deal of wisdom. The out-of-hand rejection of the possibility of such wisdom is in itself astonishingly narrow.

One of the major themes of this book is that the friendship relationship is an extraordinarily difficult and elaborate one; when it is reinforced and complicated by the partners also being man and wife, the problems increase, even if the payoff also increases. In other words, the happy, fulfilling genital relationship between one man and one woman is hard to come by. I doubt very much that the mere elimination of old-fashioned morality would make genital relationships with everyone else in the community satisfying or even feasible. *The Harrad Experiment*—and similar utopian visions—are just that, utopian, in the strict Greek meaning of the word. They are things that could happen at no place where real human beings are.

I have no doubt that in friendship communities there will be a heightened awareness of sexuality. I think this awareness will be all to the good so long as the marital relationships within the community are strong and fulfilling. If they are not, the community is going to have a great deal of trouble or, to put the matter even more bluntly, friendship communities are possible only for the very mature and self-possessed, and they are possible only for those married couples whose marriage friendship is a rich and expanding one.

The relationships, then, between friendship and society are many and complex. Society cannot do without friendships and friendships cannot do without society, although there are times when friendships mess up the efficiency of society and society impinges on the tranquillity of friends. If the myth of lover and the beloved, isolated by themselves in serenity on a South Seas paradise seems extraordinarily attractive, those who find it too tempting should ponder the thought that on their Bali Ha'i no one else would know how happy they were. Most of us, I think, could tolerate that for only a brief period of time. Happiness demands that it be shared.

17

THE FUTURE OF FRIENDSHIP

Risk-taking, as we have said, is essential to friendship, and the risk-taking never stops. For all our sensitivity and experience, for all our ability to read the signals and interpret the codes, we will take a risk when we expose ourselves to our friends. We must still make choices in the midst of ambiguous and uncertain stimuli. The more important the friend, the greater the risk because, for the important friend, more of ourselves is invested in the gift we are offering. For husband and wife, each act of loving is a renewed risk. They can never absolutely be sure that in this particular act they will be attractive and responsive enough. Each time they begin to make love with one another they, in the most literal sense of the word, put their bodies on the line, and put in jeopardy their most primordial adequacy.

The man, it has often seemed to me, risks more than his wife, because no matter how skillful they have become at sharing the roles of conquering and surrendering, he is still the one who physiologically holds the initiative. If he is to fail, biologically speaking, the failure will be more obvious and so his adequacy is more in doubt than his wife's. The two of them are risking more than their bodies in the union. If it is a relationship where there is affection and friendship, then far more is at stake in their union, since far more is being symbolized than the release of physical tension. One does not wish to argue that these fears of risk-taking are explicit or conscious or even very powerful; one simply asserts that they are there and must necessarily be there not only in love-making but in every interaction of any friendship experience.

There are so many things we cannot be sure of. Will our friend respond to our initial invitation? Will he sustain his response? Will we be able to fight the terror of our own fears? Will he overcome his own terror? Will we use the right tactics or the right strategy with him, and will he respond with perceptiveness and sensitivity to us? We cannot be certain of the adequacy of our choices nor even of the consequences that will flow from the choices. The essential anguish of friendship is its uncertainty; the strain toward escaping from uncertainty is extraordinarily powerful in the human organism, so we attempt to escape uncertainty with magic answers and pat solutions. Or we cover up uncertainty with silence or by creating a culture for our relationship in which critical issues are ignored and in which rules are established to excuse us from making demands or responding to them.

We try to make rules in order to freeze the relationship at a low level of trust and eliminate the need for risk-taking and with it, of course, the possibility of growth; or alternately, we seek the emotional orgy of some kind of sensitivity or encounter experience, hoping to achieve instantaneous solution to the uncertainties and ambiguities of friendship.

If the conspiracy of silence does not work, then perhaps the conspiracy of noise will.

So the future of friendship is a future of anguish and a future of terror but also a future of delight and a future of ecstasy. The human race may progress to such an extent that we become much better equipped to deal with the terror and much more skillful at cutting through the ambiguity. Presumably, then, the delight and the ecstasy will increase; yet it seems unlikely that the creature man will ever be completely free from terror and ambiguity, so his friendships will always involve risk-taking in uncertain circumstances. There are times when we may wonder whether we would want it any different.

We have spoken of friendship in this book as though it were between two people, though actually friendship communities can include more than two people, and in the family, in most circumstances, the friendship community expands to include children as well as parents, especially when the children move toward adulthood. An attempt to analyze the growth from dependent children to adult children who are friends of their parents is beyond the scope of this book, though it is clear that the process is even more intricate than that by which husband and wife become friends with one another.

Friendship communities beyond the limits of the family are becoming popular in the modern world as men and women try to escape from what they take to be coldness and impersonality in our bureaucratic and technocratic society. Such communities, whether they be religious or political or cultural or even psychedelic, are noble attempts that involve far more difficulties than most of those who join such communities realize. Friendship is not easy, is not automatic. It is not achieved through intense quasitherapy sessions nor through communal smoking of marijuana. The marriage relationship or a relationship with one friend is a strain on most human beings; to juggle a whole friendship network at the same time is a much more serious strain, particularly when one's marriage, somehow or other, becomes involved in that network. Now the terror that separates husband from wife is not restricted to intimacy in the home but is in public for all to see.

Friendship communities probably represent a dramatic step forward in human culture. The ability of the social sciences to begin to understand the dynamics of such communities is extremely important, but those enthusiasts who think that the problems of the friendship community are easy to solve, or even easy to understand, are only kidding themselves.

One of the extraordinary discoveries of modern society is that the key decision-making positions in the corporate bureaucracies must now be occupied not by individuals but rather by problem-solving teams, that is to say, by groups of men and women who are able to combine their skills and their access to information in a smoothly working harmony of competence. For such a decision-making team to function well there has to be some kind of basic trust among its members. They must be at ease with one another and not feel the need to compete with each other. In other words, a decision-making team must, in some fashion, be good friends. The intimacy required of such a team is obviously not the intimacy between a husband and wife or even between two close friends in a nonoccupational situation. As a matter of fact, it may well be that too much intimacy would be dysfunctional for such a decision-making team (though again it may not be, but on this subject more research is required). But there is every reason to suspect that without some sort of preliminary friendship relationship a decision-making team will simply not do what it was designed to do.

Similarly, despite the multiversity and the mass approach to higher education, despite teaching machines and computers and instructional television and other marvels of educational technology, it still seems that the most critical learning experience occurs between the teacher and the student and that that experience, if it is to be meaningful at all, involves some kind of friendship between the teacher and the student. As a matter of fact, it can be said that the teacher, by his attractiveness, actually seduces the student to learn. Surely, at the higher educational level, it is almost the *sine qua non* of learning that the teacher conveys to the student the fact that he is willing to listen to what the student thinks. If the teacher is not willing to listen to what the student thinks, it will be most difficult for the student to conclude that there is any value in his thinking. He therefore might give up thinking but instead concentrate on getting a good grade (and getting a good grade has nothing necessarily to do with thinking).

Finally, in the larger society, torn as it is by social, economic, racial, and ethnic conflict, it has become increasingly clear that unless men from diverse backgrounds are able to learn some amounts of trust, our society cannot survive. Hobbes' problem has not been solved, and in a technocratic and bureaucratic society, where various groups compete fiercely with one another for power and privilege, where the mass media make every event instantaneously available, and when the delicate balance that holds a nation together can easily be damaged, a solution to Hobbes' problem becomes more imperative than ever. There may have been a time when trust and friendship were optional for the human condition; in the modern world they are becoming essential. Friendship between black and white can hardly be expected to be the same as friendship between husband and wife or two close friends who share many values in common, though one must say that if friendship is not more widespread between husbands and wives we are not likely to have children who are capable of any kind of trust in dealing with those who are different from them. But if the relationship between people of different human groupings is not likely to be intimate, it still must involve some trust, some invitation, some promise, some gift-giving, some delight, perhaps even some faint touches of ecstasy. There is no other way that man knows to conquer terror, and terror is the root of hatred.

To put the matter more bluntly, in the modern world friendship is not optional.

And so, whether we like it or not, all of us have to learn to love one another.